from DEATH... ^to LIFE

One Man's Journey

Revised Edition

from DEATH... *to* LIFE

One Man's Journey

DONALD NALLEY

"The Lord gave the word and great was the company of those who published it."
Psalm 68:11

Cover design by Rodrigo Adolfo
Interior design by Jomar Ouano

Published in the United States of America

ISBN-13: 978-1974476824
ISBN-10: 1974476820

1. Biography & Autobiography / Personal
Memoirs
2. Religion / Christian Life / Inspirational

Acknowledgments

First and foremost, I dedicate this book to my Lord and Savior Jesus Christ who has made this work possible because He is the one who has freed me from a life of crime and thirty-two years of drug addiction. He is also the one who led me and empowered me by the Holy Spirit to write this book and my testimony. "For as many as are led by the Spirit of God, these are sons of God" (Romans 8:14).

Secondly, to my lovely wife Katie who is a gift from God and the other half of the ministry team, who is always there to support me in whatever the Lord Jesus Christ has us doing. "He who finds a wife finds a good thing, And obtains favor from the LORD" (Proverbs 18:22). I must have great favor from God because she truly is a good wife!

Thirdly, to all the church leaders out there who have been a great influence and encouragement to us stepping out into the ministry the Lord has called us to do. The body of Christ is truly blessed in this day and hour to have such passionate leaders who want to see others excel and succeed in their gifts and callings. "And He Himself gave some to be apostles, some prophets, some evangelists, and some pastors and teachers, for the equipping of the saints for the work of ministry, for the edifying of the body of Christ" (Ephesians 4:11–12).

CONTENTS

Foreword

Don Nalley's story offers hope for all who have lived a defeated life. The book chronicles a young addict's life filled with death, darkness, and deception. His story truly is a testimony to the resurrection power of Jesus Christ. God not only turned his life around, but opened a wide door of promise and possibility to many who have been touched by Pastor Don's ministry. Brought back from hell's door, Don has never looked back. He truly knows that his Redeemer lives and God has used him mightily to set the captives free.

Dr. David Thompson Chaplain,
Rock Road Jail
St. Lucie County Sheriff's Office
Ft. Pierce, Florida

INTRODUCTION

I walk into the county detention center depending fully on the Lord Jesus Christ to be with me, empowering me to preach the gospel of the kingdom of God. I'm confident He is with me to confirm His Word with signs and wonders following to bless these inmates and set them free from the things that hold them in bondages. The Holy Spirit moves through the crowd to convict the hearts of these men that there still is hope for them, that this life behind bars isn't all there is because they realize there is a God who loves them, who wants to have a relationship with them—a God of love who created them and who hasn't given up on them but is interested in them, a God who heals their bodies before they can even receive Him into their hearts. He is drawing them in with his love and goodness as if a giant magnet were pulling their hearts toward Him and they can no longer resist His love until, finally, they fully surrender to the one who laid down His life for them on a cross.

As I'm headed to a meeting and driving through a shopping center parking lot with my fiancee and another friend, I hear the distinct voice of the Lord say to me, "See that lady over there? Go lead her to Me and I am going to heal her." I stop the car and tell my friend to go and share the gospel with the lady, and we will be over to pray for her as soon as we park the car. He jumps out and off he goes on a mission for Jesus. By the time Katie, my fiancee at the time but now my wife, and I got to where our other friend was talking to the lady in the middle of the parking lot, he had already shared the gospel with her and led her to the cross of Christ. I went on to share with her that this same Jesus she had just received into her heart is a healer and a miracle worker, and he wants to heal her. I asked her if she believed Jesus could heal her, and she replied that she believed God would heal her one day. I said, "No, ma'am, you misunderstand me. He wants to heal you right here right now in this parking lot! Can we pray for you?" She said go right ahead, so we prayed and thanked the Lord for healing her, and the power of God came on her right on the spot, and she came up out of her wheelchair and started dancing in circles and giving praise and glory to God for healing her. We left her that day in that parking lot with one thought: It was Jesus Christ that saved her and healed her and that was all she needed to know. Our names weren't important. When you lift up Jesus, he will draw all people to himself...

Walking up to the podium in the church building, under a tent, or wherever God sends me, I depend on the instructions from the Lord as to what to preach and how He wants to minister through me because I am his yielded vessel through which He desires to flow. Sometimes He has me prepare notes, and other times, He just tells me to trust Him that as I open my mouth

He will fill it with His words. Other times He gives me words of knowledge about specific healing needs for people in the congregation before I even preach the Word so He can raise their faith level to receive from Him and Him alone. When I pray the prayer of faith, the Holy Spirit never fails to bless the people with signs, wonders, and miracles. I'm a faith preacher who God has called to preach the gospel of the kingdom from His Word knowing it will raise the faith level of the body of Christ so they can receive everything God has for them, but it hasn't always been this way with me.

You see I lived a very troubled life before Christ came in and intervened on my behalf, and this is my story...

In the Beginning

In the beginning of my life, God spoke and Donald was formed in his mother's womb in early 1963. Later that year, my mother gave birth to me in Washington County, Maryland. Number fourteen out of fifteen children, I was born into a good, hardworking family who lived on a farm in the Maryland countryside. I had good parents and a very humble beginning in life. I basically had everything a young boy growing up in the country could ever want —horses, cows, pigs, chickens, and everything else farm life has to offer. We had plenty of woods and fields to run around in and creeks to fish and swim in. We had bicycles, mini-bikes, motorcycles, go-carts, tractors, and wagons— you name it, we had it. I was loving life in the country especially when winter would come around and we would get a good snow. We had a field that had this long sprawling hill, and we had a 1957 Chevy trunk lid that we would sled ride down that hill on. Get about four of us on that thing and we were cruising for a bruising because you had lots of speed with no way of steering it or no way of stopping it. We usually stopped when we hit the fence at the bottom.

At the time I was born, most of my brothers and sisters were already married and had children of their own. Three of my siblings had already died, so there was actually only ten children by the time I was born. I made number eleven with just four of us living at home at the start of my life. I was the baby of the family until my little sister came along. That made five of us at home now, and I don't know what it was, but I guess jealousy got the best of me because I kind of turned just plain rotten after my little sister came along, and realized I wasn't the baby of the family anymore, getting all of the attention.

My mother was a good woman who taught me about Jesus and the plan of salvation when I was a small child, which would prove to be the very thing that would save my life thirty-two years after her death. "Train up a child in the way he should go, and when he is old he will not depart from it" (Proverbs 22:6).

My mother meant well by making sure we were at church every time the doors were open, but I just plain wasn't getting it nor was I very interested. No matter how my dad and mom tried to instruct me in the way I should go, I seemed to always do the opposite.

I would go to school and get into fights at eight years of age, steal sips of beer from Dad's beer when he wasn't looking. I had even gotten so brazen as to go through an open window on the little church we attended and took money out of the collection plate. I repented later in life for that, and the Lord has since forgiven me.

Overall I had a good childhood up until almost eleven years old. My mom had some kind of cancer that just ate away at her, and I remember we kept running back and forth to this really big hospital in Baltimore because Mom was there for a long time. Then it seemed as if she was getting better, so they put her in the same local hospital where she had given birth to me.

Eventually Dad moved us off the farm and into the city of Hagerstown to the low-income housing projects because of the massive hospital bills. He made this move while he was trying to cope with all the toll and the stress that was wearing him down because of Mom being sick.

My mother passed away five weeks before I turned eleven. After she had passed away, Dad started drinking more and more and stopped paying much attention to what we kids were doing. Needless to say, moving into a city setting a ten-year-old boy whose mother just died wasn't a very good idea. Not only did I lose my mother to cancer, but also lost my father to alcoholism, and even though he was still alive, it was as if I had no dad at all, and this was the beginning of a broken relationship between him and me.

Without the guidance of a father and with no mother, there was no one to explain to me why God would take my mother from me, so I didn't want to hear about God at all. All I knew was that my mother was gone but did not understand why, and it seemed as if I was all alone and no one cared at all, at least that's how my little ten-year-old mind perceived things.

Consequently, my mother is gone for good, my dad is drinking heavily and not caring much at all what we kids are doing, and let me tell you this, growing up in the mid-1970s, being able to do whatever you please at the age of ten, was a mixture of rebellion and destruction just waiting to happen.

I didn't hang out with kids my own age because I looked up to my one older brother who was a few years older than me, so I hung out with him and his crowd. A couple of weeks after my mother passed, I got turned on to my first taste of drugs. Here I was ten years old, getting ready to turn eleven, and the first thing I smoked was not a cigarette but hashish. I got high that day with my brother and one of his friends, right out back of our house in a small patch of trees! The euphoria and the strength I felt that day was as if all my troubles and pain went away, and I was all grown-up. I thought I was on top of the world, a big man fitting in and being accepted. Someone finally cared!

Little did I know that this one incident of smoking hash to try to cover up the pain and hurt of losing my mother would lead me down a road of destruction for over thirty-two years of my life.

THE SNARE OF THE DEVIL

I didn't realize it when I got high for the first time that it wasn't my brother and his friend offering me that hashish. It was Satan working through them to trap me into a lifestyle that would keep me numb and lost and lead me away from God instead of toward him. God has a plan for every person on the planet, but there is an enemy of God out there who wants to destroy the destiny that God has planned for you. God doesn't want to harm us in any way whatsoever, but on the contrary, He has a future mapped out for us. "For I know the thoughts that I think toward you, says the LORD, thoughts of peace and not of evil, to give you a future and a hope" (Jeremiah 29:11).

At this time in my life, I didn't know much about the Bible or how subtle Satan worked to trap the souls of people, especially young fragile people. All I really knew was that this man Jesus Christ died on a cross for my sins and would forgive me if I asked Him to. I knew nothing about true repentance and leaving my old life behind to live my life for Him, nor anything about taking up your cross and following Him. After all, I was just on the brink of turning eleven years old, and I was about to grow up faster than I wanted to.

Imagine a ten-year-old whose mother had just passed away, whose dad started to drink heavy, and all he knew was farm life in the country. Adjusting to city life was new and not so easy at first. It was a real struggle having to change schools, make new friends, and adjust to a different kind of people. I was used to the laid-back country folk and life on the farm, but these city folk were wild and lived life really fast.

Satan had my number and lured me in with something that would ease the pain of losing my mother but only lasted for the moment because, once you came down from the high, you started craving more and more to get you back up there. You always do. Without knowing it, because as I have said Satan is very subtle with enticing and drawing you in, I allowed a demonic spirit into my life that would enslave me to substances for a very long time to come.

Now that I had my first taste of drugs, I felt like a grown-up and wanted to do more grown-up things, or at least what I thought were the things that grown-ups did because of the things I was being exposed to. Everyone around me was smoking cigarettes, so why should I be any different? After all, I smoked some hashish and survived it, so surely a cigarette wouldn't hurt me since all the kids were doing it, and it seemed like the cool thing to do at the time.

So now I started smoking cigarettes and hanging out in the neighborhood where we now lived in the Hagerstown area, and for the sake of not slandering any specific areas or people from my past, I will not mention names and places where my life happened because these things aren't as important as the story of who I was and who I am now.

I'm hanging out and being cool, as I knew cool to be, and met a whole new gang of guys who spot me as the new kid in the neighborhood. They came over to see what I was all about, to try my toughness so to speak. These were the kids who did all the cool things; at least I thought they did. You know, they smoked cigarettes, did drugs, drank beer, skipped school, and lots of other illegal activity as well, but my first encounter with them wasn't a very pleasant one.

They basically came over to bully me to see if I was a pushover, which I wasn't, so I ended up getting into a small scuffle with them, but there were too many of them for me to take by myself, so I ended up breaking free from the crowd of them and running for my life to get back to my house. My one brother was with me who wasn't much of a fighter, so I tried to take up for me and him at the same time until finally we made it back to our house.

When we reached the front porch of our house, our older brother, who turned me on to the hash, came out on the porch, and these guys who were chasing us stopped when they realized that our older brother was a force to be reckoned with because he done built himself up a nasty reputation in the neighborhood as a street fighter. He would earn the nickname of "Mad-Dog" later on down the road.

Dad wouldn't let us two younger boys out so much, so these people didn't know what we were all about, but they knew my older brother well enough because he hung out with them, and I would too after this night. This was the wild older crowd I mentioned I would be hanging out with.

My middle brother was more of a daddy's boy and could do no wrong in Dad's eyes, and come to think of it, he was never in jail or prison like the rest of us boys. He wasn't a tough guy and physical fighter like the other two of us. We were the black sheep of the family and thought we were so cool because of all the devious stuff we were into. We hung out with the cool kids while he and our little sister hung out with Dad and listened to him. We cool kids would end up in one mess after another because we were really like a pack of wild dogs running through the neighborhood.

Up to this point in time I hung out with both my brothers at times, but after this incident of the neighborhood gang wanting to see how tough we were, I really just started to hang out with and cling to my oldest brother because, if something major went down, we would have each other's backs. We knew we could depend on one another to be there for each other. Our two young lives were taking a different course than that of my middle brother and our little sister. Since Mom died we were in rebellion to all authority, including Dad, and the other two weren't.

One thing I could never figure out was how my middle brother and younger sister always seemed to earn the favor and respect of our father, but my older brother and I were like outcasts. My rebellious young mind couldn't wrap itself around the concept that those two honored Dad and we didn't, so they had Dad's respect and attention and we didn't. It didn't even matter that Dad was drinking more. It just seemed to me like he favored them more than he did me. Anytime something went wrong, it seemed as if I always caught the blame and got the belt.

Now keep in mind I did have other older brothers and sisters, but they had already moved out and were living their own lives and had their own families. I will mention my other siblings in this book also, but not by name so as to protect their good reputation. Even though my family that was at home with us younger kids was coming apart at the seams, my other siblings' families weren't. As a matter of fact, our older siblings stepped in later on to do all they could to help keep the family from being divided and gave us good homes to live in.

Back to my life starting out on the streets. Once these guys who I got into a showdown with realized my older brother was one of them, I was easily accepted into their little gang of hoodlums. Here we were, the two outcasts of the family, being accepted by the neighborhood outcasts and troublesome kids. I just turned eleven years old, I'm hanging out with older guys who were between fourteen and eighteen and there were also lots of older girls in this bunch who hung around us. These girls were very flirtatious; needless to say one of them seduced me one night, and my innocence was lost forever.

The strangest thing is that it happened under one of those big drainage tunnels going under a dead end street and we got caught in the act by another neighborhood kid who was a member of our little gang. He just happened to be "passing by" at the very time we were under this tunnel. I think I was set up to be embarrassed since I was the "little boy" and "new kid" of the bunch. Nevertheless, I got over it quickly and ended up being good friends with the guy who caught me in the act. Isn't it kind of strange how you can bond closely to certain people under adverse circumstances?

This was all like an initiation for me to be in the neighborhood gang, and later on we would actually give ourselves a name. We called ourselves the "Red Devils". And boy, did we live like the devil. We were always into messes and always stirring up trouble, starting fights and destroying property, drinking anything we could get our hands on, and getting high on weed and hashish. We also were living life without rules. We governed ourselves, and no one could tell us what to do.

As time went by, I started smoking more and more marijuana, drinking more and more beer and whiskey, sniffing model car glue and contact cement, and any other kind of substances that I thought would get me high. I basically stopped going to school. We didn't play hooky. We just stopped going altogether and spent our days hanging out and getting high.

I remember one day a lady from social services came to our house to see why we weren't going to school. Well, we had the gang in the house while Dad was working, and we were all getting stoned on beer and weed. My older brother was upstairs with the members of the heavy metal band he was in, and they were just jamming away as loud as could be. We were in full party mode so us kids downstairs got the idea to clean the house, but the problem was that we were so wasted that we spilled a whole bucket of sudsy mop water all over the living room floor. Well, this made the floor extremely slippery so we do the fun thing and start slipping, sliding, and surfing across the room in the soap suds. Now just imagine the scene when I opened the door and a social services lady was standing there.

She asked if my dad was home and I told her no. Then she asked if she could talk to whomever was in charge, so I went upstairs to get my older brother who had no idea someone was even at the door since he was still playing very loud music with his metal band. When I told him there was a lady from the social services office down at the door and she wanted to see him, he did what any respectable young man would do, right? Wrong, he went down the stairs and lied straight to her face by telling her he was up there sleeping and had no idea what we were doing downstairs. She threatens to take us kids away from Dad so my brother literally called her some names I can't mention, threw her out of the house, and told her to never come back.

I'm telling all this because these are the things that shaped my view of the world around me and would govern my life in the years to come. I looked up to my older brother and wanted to be just like him. A guy who lived by no rules and took no crap off of anybody. I guess that's why we had no trouble deciding he would be the leader of the "Red Devils".

Parents, be careful who your children are hanging out with and looking up to as a role model. The apostle

Paul instructed Timothy to "be an example to the believers in word, in conduct, in love, in spirit, in faith, in purity" (1 Timothy 4:12). What or who you give your attention to the most is what you become or who you become like.

My older brother and myself would sneak out at night and party throughout the night and slide back in before Dad got up for work, but we were starting to have a problem coming up with more and more money to keep us high or drunk. We started to scheme and plan how to get cash quickly, so my brother and a couple of his friends came up with this plan to go over to the shopping mall near our housing projects and hang out in the parking lot and snatch purses from women shoppers as they got out of their cars, but it didn't quite work out as planned.

They wouldn't let me go with them because they said I was too young, so I waited in a place where I could see the parking lot and noticed after a lot of waiting they disappeared inside the mall. I had no idea they made a change of plans. I just did what I was told to do and that was to wait and not be seen by anyone. They figured I was too little to go with them, but I could watch from a distance.

Here I am just being patient and waiting when all of a sudden I see them come running full speed toward my hiding place in the woods. They got to where I was and shouted, "Come on, we have to get out of here!" We found a safe place in the woods and they told me how they figured they could get more money robbing the place instead of snatching some lady's purse so that's what they did. My brother, two other guys, and a girl robbed the theaters at knife point. These people were legends to me, and they were my role models.

It wasn't long before they got caught, and each one of them got sent away to juvenile lockup, leaving me without my older brother and best friend. I wasn't exactly on my own because I still had the gang, and we were just as mischievous as ever, and it wouldn't be long before I followed right in the same footsteps as my brother. I didn't pull any armed robberies, but I started off by breaking into cars and stealing whatever I thought was of any value I could maybe sell or trade for drugs.

I was still eleven years old at this time and was about to have my first brush with the law. I found a BB gun one day in the woods and did something really stupid with it. I shot a kid in the back of the head riding by me on a bike, and he told his parents who called the cops on me.

The police came to my house, and my dad had no idea I had this BB gun so he tells the police he don't own guns and don't let us kids play with them either. He let the police question me, and I lied to them and told them they had the wrong kid, that this kid had me mixed up with someone else. The cops couldn't do anything about it, so this just made me feel invincible like I could do anything and get away with it.

The next big caper I did was me, two guys, and a girl—sound familiar? Just like my older brother's caper. Only we broke into the neighborhood store instead of straight out robbing it. We didn't get much money, but we cleaned them out on cigarettes and model car glue, which caused me to get caught really quick. I thought we would get away with this little breaking and entering since I done had one brush with the law and got away free and clear. Boy, was I wrong.

I took my share of the cigarettes and model car glue and candy bars and other stuff home with me, and got to sniffing that glue all night in my bedroom. I passed out sometime during the night, and the next thing I know, my dad came in to get me up early in the morning and saw all this stuff from the break-in scattered all over my room. He started asking me where I got all these cigarettes and other things from. I told him some of my friends gave it to me, and wouldn't you know it, no sooner than that comes out of my mouth, someone yells up the steps that they just got back from the store up the street and it was broken into and the police were still there investigating the crime.

Dad just knew I had something to do with it, so he grabs me up and all the stuff I stole, and literally tans my hide all the way up the street to the store and marches me in there and first makes me apologize to the owners for breaking into their place of business, and then he turns me over to the police to teach me a lesson. He already had one son in juvenile lock up and now a second one headed down the same path as the first one.

They took me away and locked me up. This was the start of a long life of run-ins with law enforcement agencies. They sent me to a juvenile evaluation facility for twenty-one days so they could put me under a microscope to see what made me tick to make their decision whether I deserved time behind bars or probation. I must have passed because they gave me probation and sent me home.

Sending a young kid like myself to a juvenile lock up in Baltimore City back in 1975 didn't help shape my life for the better since, back then, they promoted smoking in these places and even gave an eleven year old boy like myself cigarettes if you didn't have anyone to bring them in to you. The state would supply cigarettes to juveniles so you could sit around and act like adults smoking and discussing your crimes with one another. One thing about this time period was they weren't much into rehabilitation. They just tried to figure out what was wrong with your head as to why you were breaking and entering at such a young age. Do their little evaluation and send a report back to the judge saying this one is normal and we think he is ready to come back home, and home you go with all your newly acquired information that you picked up from all the other juvenile delinquents you had just met.

Information as to how you got caught, how they got caught, and how maybe you could do something different the next time so neither one of you would get caught. For some reason, that's all people seem to do in these settings, talk about their crimes and what they could do differently the next time without it ever occurring to them that they got caught this time so what would even make them think they could even do something in the future and get away with it.

This is the deception of the devil that traps you into a lifestyle that leads you nowhere, and unless the system recognizes or even the individual recognizes that this is a spiritual problem and it can't be fixed by natural measures, then the person is caught in this trap or snare of a lifestyle.

We get sent to these facilities and learn more of the wrong things from one another, and we only look forward to the day we will be set free from physical incarceration, without fully understanding that only Jesus Christ has the true power to set you free spiritually. Get free spiritually and you'll stay free naturally!

But, for now, I was in the dark about all these spiritual things so I was no different than anyone else I was around, and all I was looking forward to was getting free from this facility, and my release date was approaching fast and I would finally be free! Or would I?

Free at Last but Still in the Snare

The system had mercy on me and set me free after my twenty-one–day evaluation, but here is the problem: was I really free? Sure, I was free from the physical incarceration, but I was still ensnared and in the prison of Satan's bondage. I still belonged to the devil so it really didn't matter if I was free physically because without being freed spiritually I was still trapped.

No one in my family understood these things because, after all, we weren't church-going people, and after Mom died, it seemed as if everyone in the family lost their faith in God. We no longer had time for Him. After returning home from my "big stay" in juvenile hall, Dad decided this neighborhood and the friends I was keeping company with weren't such a good influence on me, so he moved us from one housing project to another. Problem is there was the same kind of scene in this new neighborhood.

I went through the same motions of making new friends, being tried and tested by the meanest, baddest kids in the projects, having confrontations and never backing down from any of them to prove to them and myself that I'm no pushover. After all I was almost twelve years old and just got out from the big house, and I handled myself in there so surely I can take care of business out here.

It wasn't long before I found the same like-minded pack of kids to run with again, and before you knew it, I was back up to my old tricks. Dad got me enrolled in my new school, but that didn't last long because I had no interest in attending school on a regular basis, and besides, what could they teach me anyway? My education was coming from the streets, and the things I was learning seemed to get me what I wanted out of life at the time.

I started to skip school again, spending my days hanging out with my new gang of juvenile delinquents, listening to heavy metal music, which really had an influence over my thinking process because I thought life was all about sex, drugs, and rock 'n' roll. These metal bands were my heroes; and I also glamorized the motorcycle gangs of that day because I wanted to be just like them. These were the things that were shaping my lifestyle and the way I thought real life was all about.

I had no idea that I was a pawn on the devil's chess board, and I was under his influence because before long, hanging out, getting high on weed, not going to school just gave me too much time on my hands; and before you knew it, I got caught shoplifting. The manager called the police who in turn called my dad to come and get me, but my dad assured them that this would never happen again. He paid for what I tried to steal so they let me go with a warning, never taking me downtown; as a result they didn't know I was a juvenile delinquent on probation for other crimes. This made me think once again I could do anything and get away with it.

As we were skipping school one day, we were hanging out in the railroad yard, which was a big freight train yard, and we discovered that breaking into the box cars was an easy way of supporting ourselves and our gang because it was simple to get stuff off the trains. Our downfall in these crimes was the day we broke into some boxcars that were labeled with some silly name to disguise them. They were really transport cars for beer. We now had one commodity that everyone seemed to have wanted including ourselves.

We were doing pretty good by breaking into these beer trains. It made the money to buy our weed and supplied all the beer we could drink. Although one day, we just got plain sloppy. A spirit of stupid must have come over us because what we did was really stupid. Later in life, after I truly got saved, I would read the words of Jesus that says, "For there is nothing covered that will not be revealed, nor hidden that will not be known" (Luke 12:2). This means you may think you will get away with certain things, but sooner or later, you will always get caught.

We got busted on a day when not only had we broken into the beer cars, but we had also hit a caboose where we just happened to find some blasting caps for dynamite. Now we weren't sure what we were going to do with these explosives, but we took them anyway and then we hit our beer car for the day. Instead of getting out of the area like we usually did, we just went into the woods along the train yard and started drinking some of the treasure we had just stolen. Well, it was kind of cold out that day so after we got about half loaded off the beer, we decided to build a fire to keep warm. This was just plain stupid because we didn't realize we had just sent up smoke signals to let the cops know our exact location.

We were in the woods, fire blazing, guzzling beer, and getting drunk out of our minds and didn't even hear the police sneak up on us. I wasn't getting off this time with a "slap on the wrist." They took us downtown, booked and fingerprinted us, and locked us up. I was charged with breaking and entering, trespassing on railroad property, destruction of property, drinking under age, a minor in possession of alcohol, possession of marijuana, and possession of dangerous explosives.

Now wouldn't you know that it just so happened that my couple of buddies that I got caught up in this crime with were never in trouble with the law before, or I should at least say this was the first time they had gotten caught for their crimes.

There are a lot of people out there who are just like these guys. Yeah, you may have never committed major crimes or broken laws of the land, and you may be a good person at heart, but what about breaking God's laws and the Ten Commandments? I can't think of one person in the world who has never told a "little white lie". It is all evil and sin in the eyes of God, and we all will face the Judge of the universe because we all have an appointment with death one day, and then we face the judgment seat of Christ. The good news is that

God has made a way to escape this judgment, and I will explain it later on so you will have an opportunity to make a choice and decide for yourself what you want to do.

Now back to my testimony or life story as some would call it. So here I am now twelve years old, caught up in a major crime with a couple of guys who hadn't had a past record like I had. Still on probation from my previous crime from about a year before, already I had this feeling in my gut that things just weren't going to turn out so well with me this time.

We went to a preliminary hearing, and they sent me to another one of these places for evaluation before making their final decision in court as to what to do with me. As I'm down at this place, the courts decided that since these other partners in crime with me hadn't been in trouble before and their parents say that overall they are good kids, then the court decided that surely I must be the ringleader and the bad influence that had led them astray.

They each got a slap on the wrist and was sent home. I was sentenced and shipped away to a juvenile prison for boys for no less than six months, and after that I would go to a group home and finish out my time there and remain there until they thought I was ready to return home to my family.

This was a pretty heavy sentence for a twelve year old boy, not knowing if I would ever return home to my dad.

At this point in my life, I was so hurt and full of anger at my dad that it didn't matter to me if I ever saw him again because I thought Dad just plain didn't care about me anyway. I so despised any kind of authority figures in my life. I was on my own and didn't need anyone telling me what to do.

What I didn't know was that when I went away this time I would never live under my father's roof ever again. The state stepped in and deemed my father as unfit to raise children on his own because of all mine and my older brother's misbehaving, and they took my other brother and sister from Dad. They were going to place them in foster homes, but this is where the rest of our other married sisters stepped in and took them into their homes. Yeah, they got separated, but they were still with family.

Here I was starting my journey on my own in the Maryland lockup for boys, feeling like the big criminal. I would not show any fear in front of the other boys who were there, and there were hundreds of them. I even saw some old friends from my previous lockup experience, which made me feel right at home.

I wonder if a lot of those boys were like me, in that at the end of the day, when they locked you in at night and you were in your cell all alone, the tears would start to flow because you wanted answers as to why your life was so messed up and you didn't have a normal family like most kids, why God took your mommy from you and now you have no daddy either. You are tough on the outside but, inside, very deeply hurt with no answers and wondering if this is all your life will ever be. I probably spent every night like that. I was putting on a tough guy mask every day around the other guys, but every night I was just this lost, hurting little kid with no parents and no direction.

Life in this lockup was basically the same as the other, learning all the wrong things, staying away from the right things and being rebellious as ever. Finally, my six months was up, and they found me a placement in a group home in the county near my hometown.

Now this was a really good group home in that it was a Christian facility, and they didn't fail me. I just didn't want much to do with the Lord, but even at this point in my life, the seeds of the gospel were getting planted in my heart. I basically said the sinner's prayer at my interview with them because I thought it was required of me to get into this place, and they accepted me.

They took us to church regularly and taught us the Bible right on campus, but my mind was always elsewhere. I'd hear the Word being preached, but I'd walk away and totally forget everything that I had just heard. I never thought to read the Bible or anything like that. After being there a while they figured that I was safe enough to enroll back into public school. They enrolled me into the school that I had gone to before, so I got to see my old friends, and that led me back into my old habits of smoking cigarettes and weed.

Finally I got fed up with the group home and all this God stuff, so I decided to run away. I went to school one day and didn't return. I went to my old friend's house and spent the night there, drinking some beer and smoking weed. I spent the second night at another friend's home who told their parents that I ran away from the group home and their parents sat me down and actually talked to me. For the first time in my young life, I was allowed to come to the conclusion, on my own, that it was best for me to go back to the group home and turn myself into them, which I did, and they welcomed me back without any real consequences of my running away.

I finished out my time there, going to church and doing all the right things, but I never really developed a true relationship with Christ. It was just all about doing what I had to do to get through this so that I could get out of this place and get on with my young life. After all, I had big plans for myself or so I thought.

Finally the day came when I was up for consideration to be released. I had been away from my family almost a year all together, and the paperwork went through for me to be placed into a normal home, but where would I go?

COMING HOME

The day was fast approaching that I would be released, but they had to find a home for me to go to since all my other siblings were taken from my dad and placed with our older sisters and their families. I wasn't even sure if any of my family even wanted me, but one of my sisters and her husband stepped up to the plate and became my legal guardians, took me into their home, and treated me as their own son.

They also had their own son, who was only a couple of years younger than I was, so now I had a sister/mother who wanted the best for me, but I had built such a wall of hatred and anger within myself that it was hard for me to accept any kind of authority figure in my young life. I was right around thirteen years old at this time in my life and under the influence that I could do whatever I wanted, act however I wanted, and no one could tell me anything different. My mother was gone, my father didn't much care about me, and I was determined that no one else was ever going to take their place.

My sister and her husband were very good to me, and I had a normal life again in a regular stable home, but still without Christ in my life and lost as ever. Sure, my family was a good family, but not a God-fearing family. However, they lived a good, comfortable life just the same. They treated me very well and tried their best to raise me the right way, but something in me always seemed to want to go the opposite way of good instruction.

When my birthday and Christmas would come around, I would get really good things, and I remember not long after I had been living with them, they even bought me my first motorcycle and that was a "wow" for me. What did I do to deserve this? I was really a troubled kid and seemed to cause messes wherever I went. I didn't respect my sister much at first and was always rebellious against her authority and even back talking to her with things like "you're not my mother, so stop trying to take her place" and "quit trying to tell me what to do." But nonetheless they still showed me undeserved love. The problem was I just didn't accept it very well and wanted no part of this kind of love, and it was the same way I had had a problem understanding how God could love me by sending his son Jesus to die for me to take the punishment for my sins. It didn't seem like my own father cared much about me, so why should God? I was only interested in God whenever I got myself in deep trouble, and then I would call on him to help me get out of the mess. That was as far as my relationship with God went.

So there I was, almost thirteen years old and finally I had a good home, but I still had all the hurts and pains of my young past, and I still coped by burying them the same way, through drugs and alcohol. I had a good life there with my sister, but something inside of me seemed to always want to live a destructive lifestyle. Listening to the heavy metal music didn't help matters at all because when you listen to music that does nothing but glorify the devil and sex and drugs, then those are the things that you do. I thought life was one big party and we could do as we please. Who cared what anyone else thought? After all, some of my older brothers were living lives of crime also.

I was still in the same school that I had always been in because my sister lived in that district. We kind of lived in the country with a lot of wide open space, so how could I possibly get into trouble?

Well, all the friends I hung out with in school were just like me. We all had good homes, but we were hardcore weed addicts. We lived every day to smoke marijuana and found any way possible to get it. We even went as far as breaking into the trunk of the weed dealer's car and stole all of his stash, and this happened right on school property. Of course this was one big mistake because even though we got their stash, we also got beat up by them pretty bad for what we had done, and word got out for no one to trust us. That made it very hard for us to get any drugs from anyone.

Because all of this had happened, a couple of my friends and I decided that we had had enough and were going to run away from home and make it on our own. Our big plan was to pack up and just go, but how were we going to survive? Well, the only way we knew how was by stealing. We took off and broke into the same store that I had broken into a few years earlier, and then in the same night, we made our way to the railroad yard and broke into the beer trains. The only problem was that we got so drunk and passed out and ended up getting caught again.

This time when I went to court I was almost fourteen years old, and the judge sent me away possibly until I would turn eighteen. I went to this other juvenile jail outside of Baltimore City, mad at myself and mad at the world, but then again I saw some of the same guys from when I did my previous time at the other institutions. It's like we were all trapped in this life of crime and had no way out. It was not like the state didn't try to rehabilitate us. We just weren't interested in being rehabilitated.

You see, every one of us will do what we think we can get away with until we get caught. Then once we get caught, we go to whatever lengths we can to make it seem as if we're being rehabilitated just so we can gain our freedom back. We call it "playing the system" because we think we're smarter than they are.

This is where my life took another twist and opened up the door for more demons. This institution that I was in decided that they were going to take the best behaved kids with the best conduct record and grades in school on a field trip through a well known manufacturing plant in Baltimore City.

Well, one of the guys I hung out with and I came up with a plan that if we really kept ourselves in line and did really well in their school program, we would make the list and be able to go on this field trip, which would be our ticket to freedom.

We did exactly what we set out to do. We played the system and made the list—our plan worked. My friend was from Baltimore, so I figured that he had connections that could help us out once we were free.

The big day was upon us, and everything went as planned. We went on the field trip and actually did the tour of the manufacturing plant, but when we were coming out of the plant and they were loading us back on the buses to take us back to the lockup campus, the only thing that stood between us and freedom was one teacher on the sidewalk. When I heard my friend yell "let's go," that was all it took. We ran hard and fast and actually heard the other kids cheering us on as we were up and out of there. We made it, and no one even chased us because I guess, if they chased us, the others might have run as well.

We were free and in the big city. It was an adventure to me, until…well, until my friend took us to this man's house where we could stay. You see, this man liked younger boys around our age, about fourteen or fifteen years old. My so-called friend slept with him, and the guy wasn't satisfied with that. He wanted me also, and so they basically took advantage of me and had their way with me, which opened the door for more demons to come into my young life.

I guess they figured, since I was on the run from the law and didn't know anyone in the city, I would do anything to keep my freedom, but they were wrong. This guy wanted to basically prostitute me out to some of his other male friends who liked young guys with long blond hair and blue eyes, but I had had enough of this, so I told my friend that I needed to get out of this place so we took off the first chance we got and we headed to Philadelphia.

We hitchhiked all the way to Philadelphia overnight just to get picked up by the law. My friend complained that now we were going to get shipped back to Maryland and we should have just stayed where we were. That may have been good for him, but I didn't like being made into a sex slave for homosexual men. This makes me wonder today how many people out there are trapped in the homosexual lifestyle because someone forced themselves upon them at a young age. This is how Satan works, and this is how he gets a stronghold in his victims because I would be tormented by this demonic spirit in the years to come.

We are now locked up in Philadelphia and they find out we are fugitives from Maryland, so they contact Maryland and fly us back on an airplane. The whole time we are looking for a way to escape again but find none. They take us back to the lockup and put us in different housing units. I ended up doing harder time there than if I never would have run. I hated myself for what have happened to me, and I hated everyone around me. I couldn't believe God would allow me to be molested the way I was, and in rebellion against God, I started a small gang and called it Heaven's Devils. Now I was really following in the footsteps of Satan himself who was an angel cast out of heaven and became known as the devil.

Life was miserable for the rest of my time in this place because I was always getting into fights. Finally the day came for me to be released, but I wasn't exactly going home, not just yet. I was locked up in this place for about eight months, and their recommendation to the court concerning me was that I needed further aftercare before returning to society. The judge agreed and sent me to a group home for an indefinite period of time.

This time, instead of sending me to a group home close to my hometown, they sent me to one way up in the mountains over two hours away. This was another Christian group home, so it's not like I wasn't exposed to the gospel of Jesus Christ. I just went through the motions of church life and ended up only spending a year or so at this group home. My case worker worked out a deal with the court that, if I got my high school diploma, then I wouldn't have to be sent away until I turned eighteen. I could get my diploma at sixteen because they took you over into West Virginia to take the GED test. Again I put my heart into studying so I could pass this test and earn my freedom back. I was working the system and it worked.

A major problem I still had was that I was still in bondage to cigarettes, alcohol, and marijuana. We would get these nights out on the town, usually Friday and Saturday night, where they would drop us off downtown and come back and pick us up a few hours later. Some of us would get beer or weed if we could afford it and get high or drunk while we were out. Some times we would get caught and lose our going out privileges, but when we earned them back, the same pattern would prevail again.

We found a house we could hang out at where this older guy seemed to have a never-ending supply of weed, but then he turned out to be no different than the guy in Baltimore City. Because we wanted the weed really bad and he was the only person we knew who had it then, he basically took advantage of the fact that since we were from the group home and getting high, he had something to hold over our heads. For him not to turn us in, he gave us all the weed we wanted but in exchange for sexual favors, so for out of fear of losing our freedom, we did what he wanted. I believe this is also another way of how a lot of people get sucked into these lifestyles, and it is hard to break these chains once Satan has you.

The people at the group home tried everything they could to prevent me from getting high, but in the end, they figured they were trying to win a losing battle. The problem was that even though they were "good Christian people," they knew nothing about demonic strongholds and deliverance from these things, but if you keep reading my life story, you will see how God Himself personally delivered me and set me free from all these strongholds, and He can do the same for you!

The purpose of the details of my life is to show the world how messed up I was and to show how powerful the gospel and the Word of God is. The Word of God can set you free from everything you had become if you will apply yourself to meditating in it. Keep reading my story, and you will see how God Himself led me through the Scriptures and delivered me from the grip of Satan, and he will do the same for you.

Anyway the group home came to the conclusion that I fulfilled my end of the agreement by doing what the court required me to do, which was get my GED. Even though they were aware that I had a major addiction to drugs, they figured I learned my lesson about stealing and was ready to go back into society and live a normal life. They did leave me with this stern warning: "If you don't deal with your substance abuse problem while you are still young and have a chance to, it will be a major downfall and a big problem later on in life for you."

Oh, how true those words were as you will soon see. I couldn't believe that I was actually getting released and going home after almost two years away from my family. One thing was on my mind: How was I going to celebrate? Free at last and ready to go. Look out, Hagerstown, here I come.

A SECOND CHANCE

I'm finally free again and on a Greyhound bus headed back to my hometown. The group home got one thing right. I did learn my lesson about breaking and entering and stealing everything in sight that wasn't nailed down because I figured that was the thing that kept causing me to go to lockup, so if I just stopped stealing, I would be all right.

It was now 1980, I was sixteen years old, and I came back to live with my sister. I was very grateful how she put up with me because she didn't have to, but she did. It would be ten long years before I would see the inside of a jail again. Not because I was doing all the right things, but because I just didn't get caught at the things I was doing.

My sister and her husband were very good to me because I had gotten my high school diploma. They gave me a 1969 Ford Gran Torino for a graduation gift and helped me to get it on the road. I got a job with my brother, the one who never got in trouble, at a full service car wash and was adjusting to society pretty well. The location of the car wash made it easy to purchase weed as it was in a hot spot for drugs. I had the best of both worlds—a job and easy access to weed.

My drug use started to escalate, and I started to experiment with other drugs. PCP was a big thing back in the 1980s around my way, and to me it was love at first taste, so I easily got hooked on it. Also LSD was flooding our area around the same time. I loved using both these drugs because they caused you to lose touch with reality. I was dangerous with these drugs because I would take a couple of hits of the LSD and wait until I started "tripping" off it, and then I would smoke a joint of the PCP. I did this because I was hooked on hardcore hallucinating.

I would work all week just so I could "trip" all weekend. Also, I always made sure I had a stash of marijuana for every day of the week so I could get high as soon as I opened my eyes in the morning. I no longer had the drugs; the drugs had me. I felt as if I couldn't function without them.

Here I am sixteen and working. Got me a nice muscle car and I bought a decent motorcycle. I met a nice young lady, and I was loving life until tragedy started to strike hard in my family. These tragedies would catapult me into sonic speed of living life in the fast lane.

You have to understand that since I came from such a large family, all my nephews, nieces, and cousins were around the same age I was. I even have some nephews and a niece who are actually older than me. A lot of us used drugs because we did grow up in the mid seventies and early eighties when drugs seemed like the cool thing to do. Most of us had drug or alcohol addictions from an early age including my one cousin who was killed in a car wreck. He was speeding and driving under the influence of alcohol with four other people in the car, and he veered off the road and hit a big oak tree head-on, killing him instantly. He was the only one who lost his life in this accident. You would think a tragedy like this would make a person step back and reevaluate they're own life, right? Wrong. It just made me party all the more to escape the reality of it all.

Not long after this incident, another cousin of mine spent the last week of his life hanging out with me at my sister's house while they were away on vacation. We had a blast partying that week until the rest of the family came home. When they got back, my cousin took my brother's motorcycle up the road for a ride and never returns. We hear sirens in the distance, so I jump on my motorcycle and head up the road to see what's going on, and the first thing I see when I got about a mile away from our house was the motorcycle laying in the middle of the road. I had to identify the bloody broken body of my cousin that day as he laid on the street all because we were high and he wanted to see how fast that motorcycle would go. This messed me up pretty good because we didn't have helmet laws in Maryland at the time, and the sight of my relative in a river of his own blood was almost too much for me to bear. I coped with this the best way I knew how, by doing more and more drugs.

After this I met another girlfriend who partied as much as I did, because the first one didn't, so I needed someone who could "hang" with me. She also had a Christian mother, and every time I would go to her house when her mother was home, I would have this eerie feeling that there was something holy and pure about the atmosphere, and it just seemed creepy to me. The mother was a saint, but the daughter was something else altogether.

What I mean by this is that one day she got me at her house on a Sunday morning while her mother was at church, and she took me upstairs into her mother's bedroom and seduced me into having sex in her mom's bed. It was as if Satan wanted to defile the atmosphere of that place. I felt so guilty after doing that. Not guilty about having sex with this girl but where we did it. This was a woman of God whose bed we defiled.

My relationship with this girl only lasted about a year or so I guess, but it was only centered on sex and drugs. I thought she was just a little too obsessive over me, so I broke free from her. I was now eighteen years old and no longer worked at the car wash. I was working in a textile-manufacturing plant on the night shift, and by this time, I couldn't function one single day without getting high.

In order for me to keep up with the demand of drugs that my addictions put on me, because my marijuana, PCP, and LSD usage were costing me more than my paycheck could handle, I started to sell drugs to support my habits. I discovered I had a skill that I was very good at, and it not only fed my own addictions, but also made me lots of money. I wouldn't be like most drug dealers who didn't work. I would keep my job as if I was living a normal life, and no one would suspect a thing. Hey, I wasn't stealing, and this was easy money, but the only problem was that it was still against the law no matter how you looked at it. I became popular very quickly, and I finally felt like somebody.

Then tragedy struck again. One of my other older brothers who was also one of my partners in crime was doing time in a local jail. He was on work release riding his motorcycle back to the jail when a lady crossed over the center line and hit him head-on and took his life instantly. Of course once again I coped the best way I knew how, by going deeper and deeper into the hallucinogenic world of LSD and PCP to escape reality.

Not long after this happened, I met another girl, and this one would give birth to my two children. I met her through friends I partied with, so she too was a drinker and a substance abuser. We would pile into my car and head to my one other brother's house, the one who robbed the theater when we were younger, and he lived in the mountains. So off we would go every weekend because he had a lot of space, and we could party all weekend without looking over our shoulder for the police.

This was my closest brother, and he was also the first one to turn me on to the hashish in 1974, the PCP a few years later, and now I was getting ready to do another first with my older brother. I think the year was around 1981 because he died in 1982. I had my first taste of cocaine with him, and instead of snorting it for the first time, he injects me with it. I felt as if I was going to die for a split second, but then I was flying high out of that room. I liked the high, but the needle thing didn't exactly trip my trigger because I was scared I would overdose myself. So I would just get some to snort once in a while, but all that would change in the mid to late eighties when crack cocaine would come on the scene.

As I said, I would go to my brother's house just about every weekend to party and hang out with him so this one weekend in 1982 was no different. We went down on a Friday night and partied like usual, but instead of staying like we usually did, we went back home. I was getting my car painted the next morning so I had to pick up my nephew who was going to paint my car. Where we painted my car wasn't very far from my brother's house.

After we finished painting the car, we had this feeling we should go over to my brother's house, but we ignored this feeling and chose to go back home first to get cleaned up, pick up our girlfriends, and then go back down to my brother's house. It didn't work out that way. As we were at my house getting cleaned up, the phone rang, and it was one of my sisters calling to tell us that my brother had just drowned in the pond on the property near where he lived. If we would have listened to that impression to go over there first after we painted my car, then this might not have happened, so guess who blamed themselves for this death?

We kept thinking if we just would have gone there first, my brother would still be alive. Two tragedies happened out of my brother's death. One of our friends was there and tried to save him but couldn't because my brother's wife panicked and jumped into the water to try and save her husband, but she couldn't because she was so panicky that she couldn't swim very well. So this poor guy makes a choice to save the woman first and then go for his best friend who was my brother. Well, it was too late by the time he got my brother's wife out of the water, my brother had already drowned. A week after he drowned, the guy who tried to save him couldn't live with the guilt of not being able to rescue his best friend, so he blows his own brains out with a shotgun.

It seemed as if Satan would use all the hurts and pains of me losing those I was closest to to draw me deeper into the numbness of drugs and to draw me further and further away from God. Not that I was close to God or anything like that, but the seeds of the gospel had been planted in me, and these seeds would sprout up in due season as God would switch the light on. But for now, I would continue to live for myself and be my own god and live by my own rules.

The drugs just made me oblivious to all these things. They didn't make things go away because the hurt and pain was still there when you came back down to reality. So you would do more and more drugs to escape again rather than face the truth. This is the deception of drug use. You also convince yourself that you get high because you like it, but the truth of the matter is that you are in bondage and you can't stop. You can't live without the substances, but you don't want to face the reality of that conclusion, so you lie to yourself and those around you by making excuses to justify your drug addiction and that keeps you in a cycle that you can't break free from, but there is hope. His name is Jesus. He freed me and he can free you too. Just keep reading to find out how.

No Slowing Down

You'd think after all these deaths that were all related one way or another to alcohol and drugs, it would cause a person to take a long hard look at himself and make some changes and better decisions for his life. But I didn't. None of these things slowed me down at all. They caused me to put the pedal to the metal and live life full throttle toward destruction. I was in bondage and a slave to the drugs and didn't even realize it.

I got deeper and deeper into the drug game and into a life of sin. After my brother and friend died, my girlfriend and I decided that it was time for us to move in together so we got our own place and moved in with one another, having no intention whatsoever of being married. I didn't even believe in marriage because every marriage that I had ever witnessed seemed to have major problems, and a lot of them would end in divorce. I figured, why get married when you could save the trouble of divorce if you ever separated?

I never figured on having children either, but it happened. My girlfriend and I were living together. I still worked a job and was selling marijuana and getting high as ever on PCP, LSD, weed, and drinking. One day my girlfriend came up pregnant, and still this wasn't enough to slow me down. Oh, she stopped partying for the most part while she was pregnant because she didn't want to harm the baby, but not me. I sold more and more weed to make more money so we would have everything we would need for our first child. The problem was the more I sold, the more I had around and the more I used.

All my wheeling and dealing was causing a distance between me and my girl because I was always on the go trying to get more and more money. The day came in August of 1985 when our daughter was born, and she was a beautiful child, but still the drugs had such a grip on me that I couldn't stop my lifestyle of easy money and all the drugs I could do for free.

As I said earlier I was a night-shift worker, and by this time, I was working at a concrete block company twelve hours a night four days a week, so a few weeks after my baby girl was born, I thought nothing of it when my partner in crime and best friend asked if I minded if my girlfriend went out to a club with some of the crowd that we hung out with. After all, she didn't do much of anything while she was pregnant, and I was working on Friday nights.

She got her mother to babysit, and off I went to work from 7:00 p.m. to 7:00 a.m. on Friday evening, knowing she was in good hands with my best friend. To make a long story short, I came home from work about 8:00 a.m. Saturday morning, and there was my best friend passed out in my bed with my girlfriend. Both of them were naked as can be. At first I wanted to kill both of them while they were sleeping, but a voice inside of me told me that, if I did that, I would spend the rest of my life in prison. So I did the next best thing.

I took the bottle of whiskey that they had sitting beside the bed. They were passed out and didn't even know that I was there. I sat on the couch in the living room and took a long swig of the whiskey, rolled myself a joint, got relaxed, and thought about how I was going to handle this.

Finally, I woke them up, let them know how disappointed I was in them both, and basically brushed it off as if nothing had happened. I was merciful and forgiving even before I knew about Christ. As a Christian, years later, I would discover the power in forgiving others. But at this point, I was deep into sin and not living for God at all.

After this happened, my girlfriend convinced me that my friend took advantage of her and caused me to retaliate with violence by getting into a fight with him and ending our friendship. Not long after this, we moved to a different place and the same pattern prevailed. This time my girlfriend slept with another one of my friends at a party she went to while I was out working. She confided in my nephew's wife and told her the whole story, which my nephew's wife told me. I didn't say anything to my girlfriend right away but acted as if things were normal.

Then one day when my friends—my nephew, his wife, and the guy that my girlfriend slept with—were over, we were just sitting around and getting high, having casual conversation. I asked my friend, in front of everyone, including my girlfriend, if he enjoyed sleeping with her? He broke down, started crying and apologizing. How did I handle this situation? By showing mercy and forgiveness again, only this time with no retaliation. God's nature was at work in me even when I was lost in darkness, I just didn't know it.

We moved again and ended up separating for a while, but would still see one another on occasion and still sleep together, and she turned up pregnant again, so I got a bigger place for her and our kids. This wouldn't last long because now we were moving into 1987, right around the time our son was born in October of that year, crack cocaine came our way and we were meeting a whole new set of friends.

We got so hooked on the crack cocaine that, for the first time in my life, it was hard for me to keep a job, and cocaine was sucking up the profits of the other drugs that I was selling. It got to the point where we would pawn our valuables off so we could get more crack.

About this same time, my girlfriend messed around on me for the third time, and I had had enough of that, so I threw her out and told her I never wanted to see her again, and until this day I have not. I didn't have it in my heart to forgive her again back then. But through the prayers of my wife that is with me now and technology, I was able to find her on the Internet recently and forgive her and ask her to forgive me. We forgave one another and moved on with our lives.

But back then, after I threw her out, I realized that my life was going downhill really fast, so I called one of my sisters to come and get my five-month-old baby boy and my two-and-one-half-year-old girl, which she gladly did because I wanted to make sure my children were safe more than anything. Once my girlfriend was out of the way and my children were safe, I basically lost everything I had to my crack cocaine addiction.

When I hit rock bottom, I still didn't look up to the Lord. Instead I looked to the system of the world. I checked myself into the hospital detox ward to get off the cocaine and straighten my life out. I got clean for the moment, but I still wasn't delivered from the spirits of addiction.

While all this was going on with me, my sister was working on adoption papers for my children. But I would only sign for my son, not for my daughter. In my mind, my daughter was old enough so that I could care for her, but I couldn't take care of a newborn. This decision would cost me later on as you will soon see.

I went through the detox and came out clean and now had a chance for a fresh start, but would I make the necessary changes and right decisions to get on with a normal life? Lots of people were waiting to see which direction I would go. All my drug addict friends knew that I had major connections and was now single with nothing holding me back so they were looking for me to deal even more drugs. My family was looking for me to get it together and do the right thing for the sake of my children. It seems like the same pattern after my mom was gone and my dad fell off the wagon, so what would I do?

TRYING TO GET IT RIGHT

I came out of the detox, but now I needed a place to stay. So I moved in with my niece and her husband for a while until I could get back on my feet. My sister would bring my children over on the weekends sometimes so I could spend time with them. That was great while it lasted, but I couldn't stay with my niece forever. I ended up doing what I knew to do to get some fast cash. I started selling weed again, and before you knew it, I bought myself a motorcycle and moved out of my niece's house. In the process of all this, my children got divided up between two of my sisters.

One of my sisters lived down in the mountains, far away from everything, and I chose her to take my daughter, and meanwhile, my other sister legally adopted my son since I was the only one who had to sign papers. The authorities were able to prove abandonment on the part of their mother. I wouldn't sign my daughter over to anyone because I had high hopes of getting myself together and getting her back.

Also, at this time in my life, my ex-girlfriend, who had both of these children, was messing around on me, so I really questioned whether or not my son was truly mine. I didn't think so; therefore, I signed adoption papers for him, but not my daughter.

What I eventually did was move out of my niece's house and moved in with another one of my sisters who lived close to where my daughter was. I chilled out for a while on selling weed and got a job building houses. We would carpool to Baltimore City where I met my next best connection on a job site. I met this guy who asked me about some weed and I told him that where I was from I could get him all the weed he wanted. He told me weed was scarce in his neighborhood, but there was plenty of PCP and cocaine. After connecting with this guy a few times, it wasn't long before I quit my job altogether and ran after the fast, easy money of dealing drugs.

My sister, whom I was living with, got on to what I was doing and asked me to leave her house. So I did because I didn't want to bring any heat down on her. By the time this happened, I had also made a really great LSD connection. I learned how to cook up my own crack cocaine, and I was getting really known on the streets as someone who would treat you right when you needed a fix.

As I drifted further and further into the world of dealing drugs and doing drugs, I drifted further and further away from my daughter and my visits with her. I was known on the streets as someone who had whatever you wanted anytime you wanted it. The year was 1988, and I was flying high. I had so much money and such a variety of drugs: PCP, powder cocaine, crack cocaine, weed, LSD, pills—you name it, I had it. The problem was I also liked doing the drugs, and not just doing them but mixing them together and doing them.

I also got popular with the ladies, and I wouldn't be caught in a serious relationship. My life revolved around sex, drugs, and rock 'n' roll. It was like every week I had a different woman, and sometimes two at a time, and once in a while a cross-dresser would get in the mix also. That was the grip that all these different demonic spirits had on me from when I was molested earlier in life. I said earlier that this fornicating spirit would pursue me, and it did just that. I wasn't an all-out homosexual, but some bisexuality was at work in my life at times. It was something I was ashamed of— that I did secretly. This was the lifestyle I lived, and the crowd I ran with lived this way also. It seemed as if there was no way out and no where to turn to break free of all this promiscuous living.

I actually felt as if I was on top of the world because with the money and drugs came power, and I lived with the attitude "I'll do what I want, when I want, how I want, and there's no one who can stop me." I had so much money and drugs all the time that I didn't know what to do with it all. I would be so stoned at times living in the country that I would crash cars, wreck my motorcycles, and just buy other ones. It never occurred to me how blessed I was to come out of these accidents without a scratch on me or never getting a DWI for drinking and driving.

I was on top of the world and living high on the hog until something strange happened one night. I'd been up partying and got really strung out on the crack and powdered cocaine, PCP, and LSD. I think I hadn't slept much at all over a two-week period while at the same time I was doing massive quantities of these drugs. All I wanted to do was just keep getting higher and higher.

I loved to hallucinate and trip hard as we called it, but it wasn't wise to push your physical body as hard as you were pushing your mind. What I mean is that your mind can want to go, go, go; but your body is screaming: rest, rest, rest!

Anyway, a friend of mine stopped by at the farmhouse I shared with other drug dealer friends of mine. He stopped by to pick up a package of drugs and drop some cash off to me. He asked me how I felt because he said I looked drained and that my head was blood red and that I should get some rest and lay off the drugs for a few days. I kind of thought that maybe he was right. I got some rest all right but not in the way I wanted to. I didn't know that I would be resting in peace for a day or so, and I wasn't prepared at all for what I was about to experience.

TOOK A TRIP WITHOUT LEAVING THE FARM

I agreed with my friend that I did, indeed, need some rest, and I remember it was on a Friday night around eight in the evening when he left the farm. Not only that, but let me fill you in on this farm we lived on. It was out in the middle of nowhere, and the lane to get to it was probably about two thirds of a mile long, so the farmhouse itself was surrounded by nothing but cornfields. You couldn't even see it from any road at all. It was basically out in the middle of nowhere in the state of Pennsylvania.

My drug dealing friends and I leased it, and it was so big that we each had our own rooms, and if we went in our room and hung a Do Not Disturb sign on the door, then we wouldn't bother one another—that is, until this incident happened that I am about to tell you about.

When my friend left that evening, I was at the house by myself, so I went upstairs to my room to get some rest and I put my Do Not Disturb sign on my door and locked myself in. I was so tired I just lay down on my bed in my clothes, and I must have just passed straight out. The next thing that happened to me might seem unbelievable to some of you who are reading this, but believe me, I know without a doubt that what happened to me was very real, and I am just giving testimony to the truth of the matter.

Here is what happened as I remember it. I felt such a peace and a calm as if I was floating. I also knew something amazing was happening to me because I actually was floating in the air in the room where I went to sleep. Also, I wasn't alone. There were two angelic beings holding me up under my armpits, locked arm in arm with me, and I realized this is how I was being suspended in midair above my bed. There was such a peace and a love that I was feeling in the presence of these angels. I also looked first to my right at the one on that side and thought this is the most beautiful person I had ever seen, perfect in all of his features, and the one on the left was the same way. I thought, *This is totally amazing*, like, *Wow, what is happening to me?*, and then I looked down, and that's when I saw myself lying on my bed where I went to sleep. I couldn't figure out how I could be down there but was also up in the air looking at myself from my position above the bed.

It didn't matter to me that I was down there because I was experiencing such a love and peace here in the arms of these angels. As I was gathering my thoughts and just starting to realize that I must have died for my body to be down there and me to be up here, even that didn't matter because all I cared about was the love and comfort and amazement that I was experiencing. I was trying to comprehend and take all this in, and that is when I heard His voice.

I knew it was God—it had to be! He didn't speak directly to me. He spoke to my escorts, the two angels who had me in their arms. He gave them some instructions concerning me. He told them that my time wasn't up yet, and it wasn't time for me to go, to send me back because He had other plans for me. That's all He said, and they obeyed and sent me back into my body. The moment my soul went back into my body, I came back to life and sat straight up on my bed, and I knew without a doubt that I laid down on that bed and overdosed and died, and no one even knew it.

The amazing thing was the time span. When I laid down, it was Friday night, and when I awoke, it was Sunday late afternoon. Almost two whole days had passed without anyone checking on me. No one had a clue that anyone of us could lay down and die just like that.

When you are deep into drug use, it's like you push yourself to the limits and never think that this next hit could be your last because no one sets out to overdose unless you intentionally want to commit suicide. The drug addict sees it as fun and games, not something that could cost him his life.

After this happened to me, it really freaked me out enough to stop getting high, but it didn't scare me enough to realize I needed God in my life. I just didn't want to get high anymore because I didn't want to go through dying again. I thought if I didn't get high, I would be all right.

It didn't stop me from selling drugs though because drugs were my money-making machine. Finally, we all decided to let the farm go because it was getting too "hot" or well-known as a drug haven, and we didn't want to get busted and go to prison. So we all moved out on our own, and I had all but stopped dealing. I was trying to keep a low profile.

Since I straightened up a little, I started to go visit my daughter again, and then I moved in with my nephew and his family. We got my daughter from my one sister and took her in to live with us. I went to work building houses with my nephew, we had my daughter living with us, and I was loving life, but then the old demon came back and I started doing cocaine again.

Doing cocaine led to dealing cocaine, and other things happened that led to my nephew and I getting into a major fight, so I had to move out and get my own place. We moved right down the road from my sister who had raised me after I had gone to juvenile hall.

That posed a problem because now I had my daughter with me. Slowly I got sucked back into dealing drugs full-time because of all the money to be made, and I wanted my daughter to have the best of everything. It was good, I guess, that I never did the drugs around my daughter because I would take her to my sister when I went on my drug runs, but now it seemed as if my sister had my daughter more than I did.

My daughter was almost five years old when the ball started spiraling downward for me. You see, when you are living the lifestyle that I was living, you think you are invincible, but sooner or later, you always get caught. I had soon forgotten my life-after-death experience back on the farm, and it was like a faded memory in the back of my mind, so my drug use was going full throttle again. I was back selling drugs all over again and doing them too! Most of the people I dealt with I had known forever and didn't realize that I was under surveillance. One lady I knew really well must have gotten busted, and to avoid going to jail, she set me up.

She bought some PCP from me, which I thought was strange because she was a cocaine addict. What I didn't know was that she was setting me up, and it was a controlled buy. The narcotics squad wanted me, and they had to get someone close to me that I trusted to get a buy from me. After they got this buy, they didn't arrest me right away, so they could get me when I made a drug run and had much more on me because they wanted me off the streets. So they set back and followed me for a couple of months until they were sure they had me, and then they raided my house after they knew I had just loaded up. That's when they got me.

The strangest thing is that after this lady got this "controlled buy" on me, a friend told me that she set me up, so I knew it was a matter of time before they would come to arrest me. You would think that I would have stopped doing what I was doing so that more charges wouldn't pile up on me.

The definition of insanity is doing the same thing over and over again and expecting a different result. The truth of the matter is that, we are so blinded by Satan that we can't even see these things or figure them out while they are happening to us, and that blindness can only be removed by the gospel of Jesus Christ. The Bible tells us, "But even if our gospel is veiled, it is veiled to those who are perishing, whose minds the god of this age has blinded, who do not believe, lest the light of the gospel of the glory of Christ, who is the image of God, should shine on them" (2 Corinthians 4:3–4). We are just pawns in the devil's game of destroying our lives.

The date was September 26, 1990. I was twenty-six years old, and it was ten years since I had walked out of the juvenile system, and now I was about to be into bondage to the adult prison system, which will take me on a journey in and out of prison for the next seventeen years of my life.

Like I said, they had me under surveillance and were watching and waiting for me to make my move. Of course I knew they were watching me, but I thought I was smarter than them. I made a run to Baltimore to "cop" my cocaine, and they were waiting for me when I returned home. They waited until I got in my house and gave me just enough time to be in the midst of packaging up my drugs when, all of a sudden, they kicked my door in and straight up caught me in the act.

They charged me with multiple counts of drug charges. Distribution and possession of PCP, distribution and possession of cocaine, marijuana possession—they piled them on me. There were also two females with me, one of which I had just met that very day, and they charged them with all the same charges they gave me—it's called guilt by association. So be careful who you associate with, know the people whom you trust your life with.

They confiscated my car and motorcycle, my cash, and after they locked me up, they came and hit me with more trafficking charges of PCP from when the lady helped them to get the controlled buy and the ball rolling against me. They wanted to put me in jail and said I was facing a very long time. They tried to cut a deal and wanted my connections. They said they would go easy on me. I wouldn't cooperate. I basically told them to shove it and give me my time. I told them I did my crime, I can do my time. I felt like the man, and nothing they threw at me could bother me. But there was one thing that got the best of me...

STUNNED AND LEFT
IN A STATE OF SHOCK

The night they raided my house, they were after more than just to charge me with multiple counts of drug charges. Since they had me under investigation and surveillance for a while, they knew I had a daughter. So they questioned me as to where she was while I was doing all this dealing.

I told them that they didn't have to worry about my little girl because she was in a safe place at my sister's home and that I didn't do drugs around her or sell them around her, which of course they already knew since they were watching me so closely. But, still, they were hoping to take her from me. I believe they were more concerned about her safety than anything.

With all that said and done, they took me away to the county jail to book me and fingerprint me. It was really rough the first few nights because it is hard on your mind and body when you are used to putting substances into yourself and then you have none. I think I mostly slept through those first few days, only waking up for chow time.

It was at first as if I was in some kind of bad dream and was hoping to wake up out of it sooner or later. Then the reality of my situation began to sink in that I may be facing some major time here. They took me down for a bond hearing, and I was thinking that I might get out on my own recognizance or my bond wouldn't be too high, but I was wrong. They set my bail extremely high because they had me and were determined that I wasn't going to slip through the cracks of the system.

I had no one that would pay my bail for me so that I could get out, which was just as well anyway because I would have probably gotten out there and racked up more charges. So here I was having to sit in jail to await my trial date. It didn't take me long to settle into the routine of life behind bars.

My sister would bring my daughter in to see me every week, and that was the high point of my week. I looked forward to seeing my baby girl every week. Even though she was five years old at this time, she was still Daddy's baby girl. These visits were like clockwork, and my sister never skipped a beat until Christmas week.

My sister came in to see me, but she didn't have my daughter with her. She told me that my ex-girlfriend, the child's mother, came and took her. I said, "What do you mean she came and took her?" She said because I wouldn't sign those custody papers of my daughter over to any of my sisters when my girlfriend and I first parted ways, there was nothing they could do to stop her from taking the child. After all, she was the child's natural birth mother.

When I got busted, it was all over the news and in the newspapers, so even though my ex-girlfriend wasn't in Maryland at the time, others were who notified her that I was on my way to prison. So she came back and took my daughter. Not knowing where my baby girl was truly hurt me more than anything. I was crushed on the inside and didn't know if I would ever see my daughter again. There was nothing I could do but cope with it the best that I knew how.

One of the inmates invited me to go up to a church service in the jail one night, so I did. They gave me a Bible, and I said the sinner's prayer. My motive was all wrong, because I was only hoping that God would get me out of this mess that I was in. I had no real intentions of serving the Lord. I just wanted Him to serve me by getting me out of the mess that I was in. I guess I was just hoping that somehow God would just reach down from heaven and magically make everything right in my life. After all He was God!

It just didn't happen that way. After sitting in the county jail for nine months, I finally got my day in court. I was feeling good since I was a first-time offender as an adult, and they offered me a plea agreement to plead guilty to one count of possession with intent to distribute cocaine, and if I did that, they would throw out the rest of the charges. So that is what I did without realizing that I could still get a lot of time for this one charge.

A lot of my family members showed up in the courtroom that day. It was June 17, 1991, my sister's birthday. I thought this was a good sign. My case was heard, the plea deal accepted, and now the judge was about ready to sentence me. I was feeling great. The judge looked at me and said, "Mr. Nalley, I don't believe you just started dealing drugs yesterday. I believe you have been selling drugs for a very long time and that you just haven't gotten caught until now. As a matter of fact, in my eyes, you are no different than a murderer because for all I know you could have sold someone something and they could have died from it." My belly started doing flip-flops at this statement, and it was as if all the life was just sucked out of me in that moment.

Then he sentenced me fifteen years to the division of corrections. I was waiting for him to say "fifteen years all suspended," but there was none of that, just fifteen years, and the gavel came down. I believe everyone in that courtroom was just as stunned and shocked as I was. Fifteen years and I'm up the creek without a paddle. I went back to the county jail for a couple of more weeks, and then they shipped me to the division of corrections. First stop is the diagnostic center where they determined your security level. Mine was medium, so they sent me to a medium-security prison about three hours from my hometown even though there was a prison in my hometown not too far from where my sister lived. I guess they do this because they don't want you to be comfortable.

I settled into prison life pretty easily, and once I saw how things were set up and the programs were run, I decided that I was going to do all I could so that I could have a good conduct record while I was behind bars. These conduct records help you when you go up for parole, and since this was my first time in the prison system, I had a good shot at making parole my first time up.

Since my charge was considered a nonviolent crime, I would be eligible for parole in about four years unless I could get an appeal or something. It seems as if everyone who goes to prison gets their time for their crime and then they spend their time trying to appeal their sentence, so why should I be any different? I filed for some kind of post conviction on my plea agreement and then got on with my time.

In the meantime, I was able to get a transfer after a few months and was shipped to that prison near my sister's home, so she could come visit me. I also started going to church services regularly, and since I had all this time on my hands, I decided that I was going to read the whole Bible. I didn't have any real relationship with God, but I still would read the Bible more or less because there wasn't much else to do once you were locked in for the night.

The only problem was that I had more of myself still wrapped up in who I used to be than in God. I was reading the Bible as any old book, not as if it was God's own Word. I would read the Word, go to church, come back to my cell, and get high. Just because you are in prison doesn't mean you can't get what you want. I was still smoking cigarettes, marijuana, snorting cocaine, and smoking PCP on occasion, and all this while I was serving time.

You see, I still had the mentality of playing the system or getting over on the system. On paper, it looked as if I was a top-class model prisoner, but on the inside of me, nothing had changed at all. I was still trying to figure out what mistakes I had made in my drug-dealing business so that I could correct them and not make those same mistakes once I got released.

Not only did I attend church services regularly, but I also got involved in the various twelve-step, self-help programs that the prison system had to offer. Again, I really had no strong desire to be clean, but I thought by doing all the right things it would help me out in the long run and look good on paper when I went up for parole. I was doing the same thing I learned in the juvenile system; I was "playing the system."

I also took auto mechanics and became a shop aide very quickly and was ASE certified, teaching others how to work on vehicles. As a result, my life behind bars wasn't so bad. I tried to keep to myself and avoid trouble at all cost. I got along with everyone.

Now you might ask, how could someone read the Bible but not draw close to God? Because to me God was someone who would come and rescue me every time I got myself in a mess, and as far as I was concerned, He had helped me to only get fifteen years instead of about one hundred, so the problem was solved. I thought that as part of being a Christian, it was your duty to go to church and read the Bible. It was something you had to do, not something you enjoyed doing. I was mostly doing it to pass time. I didn't get much out of it. I was just going to church to get time out of my cell and be entertained.

Almost three years had gone by, and I had basically forgotten about my appeal when they granted it to me. They took me back to court and reduced my sentence down to ten years with the recommendation that I also get paroled. So now I was on my way out the door. In all it still took about nine more months for me to get released, and in between that time, another bombshell was dropped in my lap.

I got a visitor from child protective services who told me that my daughter had been taken from her mother and was now a ward of the state, the state of Arizona, that is. Here I was in prison in Maryland and my daughter was about to be adopted by strangers in Arizona. I had failed as her father and feared I would never see her again. I just wanted to go into the pit of drug use to cover over the sting of pain from this, but my freedom was on the line, and I sure didn't want to get any dirty urine samples between this time and my parole hearing. I decided to keep my nose clean and tough it out.

I went up for parole, and they went by what the judge recommended and paroled me right away. I had done three years and nine months on a fifteen-year sentence that got reduced down to ten years and I had six years and three months to complete on parole, to keep my nose clean and stay out of trouble. Would I be able to do it?

Out but Not Free

As always, my same sister was there for me to pick me up from the prison when I got released. She also took me back into her home so that I would have a place to live until I was able to stand on my own two feet. I also had a job lined up with my nephew going back to framing houses. They started me out at carpenter's wages, so not only did I have a place to live, but I had a good job with good pay to go along with it. One of my brothers-in-law gave me a 1965 Chevy pickup truck that needed a little work done to it. So I took it and did what was necessary to get it on the road.

Life finally seemed as if it was going in a right direction for me. I had to report to my parole officer every other week, and I had to go through the county's drug rehabilitation classes. I also had to go to a twelve-step recovery program meeting once a week and give random urine samples so they could monitor if I was getting high or not.

Yeah, life was sweet, until I ran into some of my old connections. The lure of the quick, fast cash was too much for me. I fell for it hook, line, and sinker. Before you knew it, I was selling drugs within a year after I had gotten released. Oh, I kept my job because it was a stipulation of my parole that I had to work, but I still thought I could beat the system and outsmart them. At first I wasn't getting high at all, but then I guess I thought just one time wouldn't hurt me. Boy, was I wrong, because that one time kicked my drug addiction back into full force.

I met a young lady through one of my old connections, and eventually we started dating. She was nineteen and I was thirty-one. She was having trouble with housing and an ex-boyfriend, so I wanted to be her knight in shining armor. I helped her out, and eventually we got our own place and moved in together. Living a life of sin doesn't cut it in any relationship especially one that revolves around lust and heavy drug use. Although my drug use was casual, I had a young girlfriend who just wanted to party all the time. So eventually I started doing more and more drugs myself. We were big into PCP and crack cocaine, and then we tried heroin together for the first time. At this time in my life, I didn't like heroin that much so we didn't do it too often.

One thing about this young girl was that she was very manipulative, and she started running around with an ex-boyfriend whom I got into major fights with on occasions. Well, when I realized she was messing around, I started having safe sex with her by using condoms. There is no such thing as safe sex unless you are married. It is all sin outside of marriage. Anyway she turned up pregnant and I told her it wasn't mine. She demanded that I pay for an abortion, or she would turn me in to my parole officer for getting high. So I gave in and this happened twice. Two abortions I was forced to pay for because of my bondage to drugs. I didn't know how to break free from the drugs or her until I met her twin sister. Her twin sister and I got along very well, and she would become my closest friend.

Her twin sister told me that she controlled all the guys she'd ever been with and usually they ended up in jail. This girl went as far as have some trumped-up charges of assault and battery put against me, and they came and arrested me. My brother paid my bail to get me out, and I had no intentions of showing up for this court date because of me being on parole. To make matters worse my parole officer was notified.

I got called in by my parole officer to give urine samples, which I knew were dirty, and my parole officer asked me about the new assault charges I now had. I left the parole office that day scared, so I decided to go on the run because I didn't want to go back to prison. The only problem was that I was a real crudball in that I took off and went on the run with her twin sister.

Being on the run wasn't as glamorous as I thought it would be because, after a while, our money was running short, and I was afraid to sell drugs. I had a parole violation warrant issued for my arrest and a warrant for jumping bail, so we did whatever we could do to survive. We were basically living on the streets and eating at soup kitchens whenever we could. Then one day, I called an old buddy that I had met while I was in prison and told him that I had messed up my parole, so he helped us to get to South Carolina where my new girlfriend, the twin sister of my old girlfriend, had some connections.

We got on a bus and headed south. We got to South Carolina right near Myrtle Beach and settled in with her friends. I got a job building houses. Of course I was being paid under the table tax free, so that no one could trace me, and I settled right into my new life. I went by my middle name and was in a place where no one would recognize me. Party life on the beach was good for about a year until they caught up with me. I actually kept a low profile while I was in South Carolina, working every day through the week and partying on the weekends.

My girlfriend went back to Maryland after about three months, but I had no intention of ever going back. I didn't communicate with my family or anyone at all from my past until this girl went back to Maryland. I kept in touch with her and others through her but my mistake was I bragged to people about how slick I was by staying hidden from the law and not getting caught. Well, when people are desperate for money, they will do just about anything to get it.

Somebody in Maryland found out where I was because of my bragging and they told on me. Since I had jumped bail when I went to South Carolina, the bounty hunters and my brother offered a reward for me. How quick some of your friends will sell you out for a few dollars. One day the bounty hunters showed up at the place I was living and knocked on the door, and I just happened to be the one who answered the door. I was caught in a snare and had nowhere to run. Since I was cooperating with them and not trying to run from them, they let me pack a bag of my own clothes to take with me. I knew they had me and they knew they had me, so why not let me take some of my own clothes?

However, I took a big chance when they picked me up because I had just bought a nice little amount of powder cocaine, and I took the chance of getting more charges because instead of disposing it when I had the chance, I hid it in that bag of clothes and I smuggled it the whole way with me back to the Maryland jail. That was really stupid of me because I could have gotten new charges and more time. Needless to say, I didn't get caught, but I did get high as a kite once I was in the jail and left alone to myself. That's how powerful a hold this stuff had on me that I was willing to risk more charges and more time for the sake of one last high.

Now I'm back in Maryland awaiting trial. I went to court for those trumped-up assault and battery charges, and all the charges were dropped against me. My parole was still violated for not reporting and all, but they only kept me for about six months and then paroled me again. So two and one half years after I initially got released, I was back in for a parole violation, quickly processed and right back out, but would this slap on the wrist be enough to get my attention and straighten me up?

Oh, it straightened me up for a short while, but the same pattern would prevail. I got out, started working again with the same people as I had before, and started dealing drugs again. With a lot of people, it is hard to break free from selling drugs because of all the cash you can make in a fast, short time. So now I was out, wheeling and dealing and doing my own thing again. Getting rich quick and running over anyone who would dare to try to stop me.

I was very bad and evil as ever. If you owed me money and were avoiding to pay me, I would kick in your door with some of my boys and get what belonged to me. I'd been shot at, had all kinds of dudes pull guns on me, and threaten my life because I was taking their business, but none of these things slowed me down. It didn't matter to me if I lived or died or went back to prison; nothing could stop me. I lived a life of anarchy, no rules and anything goes. I lived for me and me alone, and no one was going to tell me what to do. I had plenty of cash, drugs, and women—what else could I want?

My freedom was cut short. I got busted again, but this time for selling heroin and cocaine, and I got caught up in one of the biggest roundups of drug pushers in the history of Washington County, Maryland. About twenty-eight of my friends and I were all rounded up by state, local, and federal authorities; and we were all in jail at the same time, facing numerous drugs and weapons violations. The year was 1999, and now I was facing my second major felony of drug charges, just short of five years after being released the first time.

MAD AT GOD

I went through the process of being booked, charged, and all the other benefits that come along with that procedure. By now I was getting used to this routine. I think because they rounded up so many of us in this sting operation, it was actually a blessing in disguise. The jail was so overcrowded that they were glad to get us all speedy trials and get us on our way to the prison system, especially since most of us were repeat offenders. And since we were repeat offenders, we were glad to get up out of the county jail also. County jails have minimal movement, but with prisons, there is more freedom.

I had my day in court and came out really well, I thought, for still being on parole. The judge gave me fifteen years, all suspended except eight years and to run concurrently with my old sentence. That meant that I had an eight year sentence with parole eligibility after two and a half years served. So now I went back to the division of corrections and got into the flow of doing my time, only this time there would be no appeal. I had gotten my time, so now I would have to live with it.

Once I got back to the prison, it was just a matter of time before I would be back to the same old stuff. Getting high when I could, getting more tattoos, and breaking as many rules as possible. I was mad at myself, mad at life, and mad at God. Some of the Christian inmates tried to get me to come to church, and I would always tell them no whenever they asked me, but I was getting tired of this because I didn't want to hear anything at all about God. I felt as if God had let me down because I was stuck in this miserable lifestyle, and there was no hope for me. He didn't get me out of prison and make things better for me the last time, so why should He now? As a matter of fact, I even thought He let my daughter get adopted by some strangers all the way on the other side of the country. I was in total rebellion against God and anyone who represented Him.

After a while, I got tired of these Christian inmates trying to get me to come to church, so in an answer to them and my rebellion against God, I put this big pentagram with a devil's skull above it on my left inner bicep. When they would try to talk to me about God or try to get me to come to church, I would pull up my shirt sleeve and show them this tattoo and say, "You see this tattoo? It represents the devil, so do I look like I'm trying to hear anything about God? Get away from me and just leave me be," I would tell them. Then I would say things like, "I tried to do the God thing the last time I was locked up, and it didn't help me at all, so why would I want to do that again?" My perception about God was all wrong. I wanted to bring God into my world, but God wanted me to come into His kingdom, and because of this, I thought God had failed me and that the church thing just wasn't for me.

So now, here I was doing my time and just passing it from day to day, waiting for this ordeal to be over, thinking that no programs or church or anything could help me this late in the game. I was basically allowing myself to be warehoused like a piece of old forgotten furniture in a storage unit. I was not beating myself up or anything like that. I was just waiting for my day to come to get released.

One good thing was that I did make it to minimum security and work release this trip around after I did about two years. I do clearly remember where I was on September 11, 2001. I was on work release doing construction on a small road bridge when our boss came out to the job site and told us what had happened to the twin towers in New York and the other things that had happened. I doubt that I would remember these things if I hadn't been in prison at the time, because I probably would have been so high somewhere that it would have been just a blurred memory.

About one year later around Thanksgiving 2002, I was getting released. I bought a car while I was on work release, saved a bunch of money, and was ready to go. I got released and went back to my sister's house to live at first, which was a good thing. I kept the same job I had while on work release for a few months after I got out, but then I ended up going back to work with my nephew and the same guys I had worked with before. That may have been a mistake even though the job gave me five more dollars an hour than where I had been. This bunch of guys liked to smoke weed, and I got drawn back in once again.

It didn't matter that I just did a little over three years again in prison and was on parole having to take urine tests regularly and in a twelve-step program. You just don't think about these things when you have a demon on your back that has you enslaved to substances. Nothing matters but what that demon wants to do. I was out, free, and starting to get high again. This was not how I planned things.

One day, I don't even remember how it happened, but I ran into the twin that I had gone to South Carolina with, so we ended up back together, and before long, I moved out of my sister's house and in with her. We started doing crack cocaine more often, and the more I got addicted, the less careful I became when having to take urine tests. So I started to get dirty urine test results again, and to avoid getting more and more of them, I stopped reporting to my parole officer all together and went into hiding. I also started injecting heroin around this time and got to the point where I couldn't live without it. I was able to hide from the parole people for a while, but then I got caught, for just a parole violation—no new criminal charges this time.

When they caught me, I was desperate and in bad shape. I had a change of heart about God so I cried out to Him for help and let Jesus back in. I started moving toward Him and doing the right things. Somehow I knew I'd just get another slap on the wrist from the parole board, and I did. I only ended up doing about six months or so. There were so many parole violations and incarcerations that I haven't listed them all, but these I have so you can see how my life was caught up in this same cycle, and it's not just me, but there are many others out there now even reading my story and wanting the answers of how to truly get free. You will see how I got totally free step by step, if you just keep reading.

I went back on a parole violation, cried out to God but somehow got back out and fell right back into the same scheme of things. I didn't plan on backsliding, it just happened. You see, I had gotten a taste for heroin before this incarceration, and now I couldn't live without it. So when I got out, I went looking for it and knew where to look. The year was around 2004, and I didn't have much time left on the fifteen-year all-suspended-but-eight sentence, so I wasn't much concerned about getting another parole violation as long as I didn't get any more new charges.

I got hooked up with this guy and girl shoplifting team. All I had to do was drive them from store to store, and they would steal certain things and then I would drive them to Baltimore to sell the stuff to certain vendors. Afterwards, they would buy heroin and pay me in drugs and cash.

I thought this was a good setup because now I didn't have to sell drugs anymore and take a big chance of getting caught. The only thing I didn't take into account was that I could still get charged with possession with intent because of how many drugs they were giving me. Also, I could have gotten charged with accessory to theft for driving them around. During this process, I also got hooked back up with my same twin girl again, who had her own place, and she was glad to have me and my newfound heroin supply back in her life. Consequently, I fell into the routine of daily heroin and crack cocaine usage and not reporting to my parole officer. The heroin usage was now getting heavier and heavier, and we were getting more and more careless. Because of this, I was about to have a date with death for the second time in my life, and it wouldn't be as lovely as the first time.

A Date with Death

Before I go into this account I would like to warn you that I truly thought that I was saved and on my way to heaven. The last time my parole had been violated I truly had a change of heart about God, and I had received Jesus back into my heart as my savior. I also had been going to church in the prison and had even gotten baptized. I had been studying the Bible and even had some awesome experiences with the Holy Spirit, so I wasn't ignorant about some of the things of God. The one thing I had failed to do was get involved with the church once I had been released, and because of this, my heart had slowly slipped away from the Lord, and that was what had led me to go after the heroin and meet this bunch of people that I was now hanging out with, who were supplying my girlfriend and me with it.

I had received Jesus as my savior, but I truly didn't make Him the Lord over my life, and I was still giving in to the cravings of my flesh. I wanted the best of both worlds, and it just can't work that way. So now, I was back out of prison trying to stay out of trouble but still wanting to hang onto my heroin habit. I fell back into the relationship with the same twin I'd been with on and off now for like ten years and connected with the people who stole to support their heroin habit. I wasn't doing a good job of keeping myself straight. As a matter of fact, I had also completely backslid from God.

Now came the most horrible, terrifying experience I had ever had in my entire life. I had just taken my friends on a run to Baltimore and dropped them off and came over to my girlfriend's apartment. We went in and sat down on the bed and shot up the heroin. In other words, we injected it into our veins. The one thing you have to understand about street drugs is that you never know how potent or powerful they are. Even though you may do the same dosage you are used to doing, if you get some really pure stuff, it can cause you to overdose and straight out kill you. I believe that this is what happened to me that day. I didn't do any more than what I was used to doing, but it must have been some really potent stuff because as soon as I shot it, I passed straight out. That is what the effect of heroin does—it causes you to nod out in a sleeplike stupor. Only this time not only did I nod out, I believed I was overdosing and dying.

When I fell out and I died, it was like the last experience. My body was dead but my soul was alive. I was fully conscious of what was going on. The moment I fell out and died, there appeared from the bottom of my feet nothing but blackness. I could still see to my left and my right that the room was normal and my girl was laying there passed out beside me, but from the bottom of my feet, it was as if someone had erased the room, and it was like staring into the deepest darkest recesses of space itself. Then this thing came out of the blackness and grabbed me by my ankles and was pulling me in there into the dark, and somehow I knew that if I got pulled all the way in there, there would be no returning for me. This was a demon straight out of the outer darkness, which I will explain later, sent to collect my soul. This thing was the most hideous beast I had ever seen. It was as black as blackness itself, and its face was like a cross between a sickly looking Doberman Pinscher and a bat with rabies. It was very muscular and had arms like a man but a chest like a dog, and it had very long clawed hands and fingers, which clamped both my ankles with lightning speed to pull me into that darkness. It had pointed ears and glowing yellow eyes. The fear and the terror it radiated was bone chilling.

You should understand that as a drug dealer and user, I had been in some very sticky situations where I had been shot at, had guns stuck in my face, been robbed, been in some nasty fights, had knives pulled on me, and all kinds of other crazy stuff, but none of these situations came close to the fear and terror that I was now experiencing.

This fear came from the inside out, not from the outside in. It was pure terror, knowing I was dying and on my way to hell. This demon pulled me in up to my knees the first time, and I don't know how, but I came back to life and was wide awake. I shook my girlfriend awake beside me and told her not to let me fall back out because, if she did, I was going to die and go to hell. She said, "Man, you are just high, so just let me be so I can enjoy my high." She didn't even bother to open her eyes to look at me. Then within minutes I fell out again, and it happened all over again. The wall of blackness, the demon, the terror, but this time he got me in up to my waist. The farther I went, the more the fear and terror increased. Then, I came back for the second time and tried to get my girl awake to tell her not to let me nod out anymore because, if she did, I would die and be lost forever. She basically ignored me again.

The heroin was too strong. I couldn't keep myself awake, so I fell out a third time, and this time the same thing happened, only the demon pulled me clean in up to my chest, almost to my neck. A little farther and I would have been gone forever, never to return. Somehow I came back to life again, but the terror of this time was almost more than I could bear, and it carried over into this natural realm we live in. This time when I woke my girlfriend up I was very bold when I said, "Listen to me and look at me because I am telling you not to let me pass out one more time because, if you do, I am going to die, and I will be lost forever. I have not been living right and I am not right with God, so if I overdose and die here today I will go straight to hell!"

This got her attention and she finally rolled over and opened her eyes to look at me, and after one look at me, she said, "You are very serious, aren't you?" I was now sitting up on the bed with my knees pulled up to my chest with my arms wrapped around them, and I was trembling all over, my eyes wide open in terror, and all the blood looked as if it was drained clean out of me because I was as pale white as flour.

I told her, "Yes, I am serious and I've been serious all along, and this is no joke and no nightmare!" I knew what had just happened to me was very real.

After this had happened, I started to cry out to the Lord, which I will get back to in a minute, but first I want each and every person who is reading this to understand something. Out of these two life-after-death experiences, one thing I do know is this: that while these things were happening to me, I was very aware and conscious of what was going on with me. In 1988 when I was caught up with the angels and in the presence of God, I experienced peace, love, and an amazement that was out of this world, and I could have gone to where God was because it didn't matter to me if I came back.

Now, here near the end of 2004, when I got snatched by this demon, it was pure evil and intense fear, such a thickness of terror that it was tangible. I was so scared out of my wits that it wasn't even funny. I didn't fully go into this pit of blackness nor did I want to, and I don't want anyone else to go there either. This is why after this happened I started crying out to God to help me, to save me, and help me get free of these drugs. I couldn't stop the heroin cold turkey because the withdrawals can kill you. I had a friend die like that.

So to keep the side effects and the sickness away I kept using the heroin, but in small dosages. However, it was different this time. I started going to a small country church even though I was still getting high. I was now crying out to the Lord to help me. Oh yeah, I would shoot heroin and off to church I would go.

God knew my heart, and I was seeking Him for His help. The people at this small church didn't condemn me for the condition I was in but only showed genuine love and concern for my well-being. You want to win someone over to the Lord, just love them. Who can resist that?

The Lord heard the cries of my heart and came through and helped me but not like I thought He would. Not long after the overdose situation, the girlfriend that I was staying with got paranoid about having a parole violator staying with her, but this was God at work. I think it was right around February 2005 that she went to her parents' house for the day, and I guess told them what was going on with me hiding out in her apartment and that she was afraid she would get into trouble for harboring a fugitive parole violator.

I think her parents talked her into turning me in, or they turned me in. Either way, it doesn't matter, because I now see it was God answering my cry for help. I was sleeping on the couch when all of a sudden I heard the keys turn in the lock, so I thought she was coming home, but I was in for a surprise. It was the police. They called out my name and said they had a warrant for my arrest. I identified myself and complied with them. I told them they had me, so let's go on to jail, I was ready. But first they asked me what were my original charges that I was on parole for. I told them distribution of cocaine and heroin. That's all it took, they started searching the place.

I told them they had no right to search this place because it wasn't my place and they didn't have a search warrant to search and seize. I said, "You have a body attachment warrant to pick me up and you have me in custody, so let's go." They didn't comply. They ignored me and kept searching. They asked me what belonged to me, so I told them. They searched my belongings and found nothing, but then they started to search under things and inside the closed coffee table, which was illegal without a search and seizure warrant. The only thing that would warrant a legal search of this residence would be if something was sitting out in the open where they could visibly see it, but there wasn't, and still they kept searching because they were determined to get me off the streets for good.

Then they found what they were looking for: some packages of crack cocaine, packages of heroin, and drug paraphernalia, syringes, and crack pipes. They took me away, and as they were taking me out of the apartment, I looked up the street just as they were shoving me into the back of a squad car, and I could see my girlfriend and her dad sitting in his car watching the whole thing go down.

I was glad it was finally over and that I wouldn't have to look over my shoulder anymore. On the other hand I was mad that they turned me in. However, I have forgiven them. An amazing thing happened on the way to the jail. Instead of taking me to the county lockup and charging me with new drug charges, they drove me to the division of corrections and turned me over to them for my parole violation. The reason they did this was because they told me that even though they found drugs in the apartment where they arrested me, they weren't going to charge me with anything because I was already in enough trouble with the parole violation. So they were just going to turn me over to the state prison system. They did just that, but would they stick to their word and was I really in the clear from getting any more new charges?

Forsaken but Not Forgotten

I was turned over to the state prison in Washington County, Maryland, where I would be put in an isolation cell until they could take me down to the Division of Correction Diagnostic Center in Baltimore. I was so relieved that they didn't give me any new charges, and I thought this would be another in-and-out thing as the system was so overcrowded. I heard they were processing parole violators very quickly who didn't have any new charges and sending them back out the door in as little as three weeks.

My time went fast because I slept through the withdrawals, and finally, they came to take me to Baltimore. I was on my way to get this little ordeal over with, but there was something that was really nagging at me. I was determined to get answers as to why I was on my way to hell after I had received Christ back into my life. I couldn't wait to get to DOC headquarters and get settled into a cell so I could put in a request slip to get a Bible because I had enough sense to know the answers that I was looking for would be in the Bible, but the answers I was seeking would be a while in coming.

For now I got settled in and focused on rededicating my life to Christ and His Word, so I started reading the Bible, but I didn't know too much about meditating in the Word. I just started at the beginning and read clean through, just casual reading, and as I was doing this, I believe this was the beginning of God starting to put a desire in me to preach the gospel even though I wasn't all the way delivered from my past self yet.

I know I was starting to get an urging in me to share my faith with others, and even though I didn't know much about His voice, it was as if something was leading me on the inside. I was really thinking now that I was clean and off the drugs and I would be all right. I'm reading the Word of God and going to church mainly just passing time waiting on my parole hearing.

The first thing they do is call you down and go over your violation with you and let you know what they are going to recommend to the parole board as to what they think they should do with you.

Well, my day came, and I went down to see them, and my hopes were very high because all I had was this little old violation of a dirty urine and a couple missed report dates. Surely they would recommend that my parole be reinstated. I was excited. I'll be going home soon. Within three weeks, just like clockwork. I went in to see the parole representative and she says, "Mr. Nalley, I see you had a dirty urine for cocaine and heroin, and you missed a couple of report dates with your parole agent. That's not so bad at all, but do you have any new charges?" I said, "No. No, I don't." She spun her file around so I could read it and she says,

"What about all these drug charges from Washington County, Maryland?"

My mind went into panic mode. I couldn't believe it. The police officers betrayed me. They forsook me. A bombshell was dropped right on my lap. I tried to explain myself. I told her that I got picked up in a house where they found drugs, but they never charged me with anything and that they weren't going to. She looked at me and said as casually as could be, "Well, they did charge you, and here is your copy of the charges, and you won't be having a parole hearing until after these charges are resolved. Send in the next man, please." I couldn't believe it—I felt betrayed, hurt, and broken. They charged me with possession of cocaine and heroin, possession with intent to distribute cocaine and heroin, and possession of drug paraphernalia.

This would be my third time for major felony drug charges, and in the state of Maryland, it carries a mandatory twenty-five years with no parole sentence. My mind was racing because of the seriousness of the situation. I was adding up the years in my mind. It was the beginning of 2005, and I had just turned forty-one years old two months earlier. I added it up, and I figured I would be sixty-six years old by the time I got out of prison. This would be like a life sentence for me.

This couldn't be happening. After everything I had just been through with dying and almost going to hell, to that place of blackness. Wait a second, God had mercy on me and spared me from that, so He could spare me from this too! I stepped out into the hallway after seeing this lady, and after the initial shock it had on my mind, I was finally starting to think clearly. Even though I was very hurt and the tears were welling up in my eyes, I pulled it out of me somewhere to tell the Lord, "Jesus, I pray that you get me out of this mess and that I don't have to do all this time, but if it is your will for me to stay in here for the next twenty-five years, then I will tell as many of these inmates as I can about you and snatch them out of the kingdom of darkness and bring them into your kingdom."

I spoke out of a broken heart, and God was about to answer me in a big way once I got back up in my cell and was all alone. I understood nothing about the fear of God, but I was about to learn real fast. Once I got back upstairs and in my cell, I started to look over my charge papers again and still couldn't believe my eyes and the police report that went with it. They were using my girlfriend against me. She was their star witness. She told them she had no knowledge of me having drugs or even doing them. This girl, who I had partied hard with for the past twelve years of my life, was betraying me. I just couldn't believe this was happening to me all over again.

How quickly people sell you out when their own freedom is on the line. Everyone including my own family turned their backs on me. Everything and all hope was removed. I had nothing left and no one to turn to except God. I found myself at rock bottom and in a hopeless situation. I was feeling betrayed and hurt all over again, so I turned to God again. Only this time I said a prayer to Him that He had heard me say time and time again when I had no one else to look to but

Him. This was my "come to my rescue and get me out of trouble prayer."

    I'm sure I'm not the only person who has done this, but I tried to cut a deal with Him. I said, "Lord, if you get me out of this mess I'm in, I promise that I'll do right by you." Surely, God wouldn't let me down, too. He wouldn't forsake me or forget me like everyone else had. After all, He always seemed to come through for me in the past when I said this kind of prayer, but would He now?

DEAL OR NO DEAL

Facing twenty-five years with no parole, I was trying to cut a deal with the Creator of everything. What I didn't understand was that I was trying to bargain with God for something that already belonged to Him, and that was me. I was trying to get His attention by having Him respond to my need in a hopeless situation, but He was trying to get my attention by allowing me to be in this hopeless situation because if He rescued me quickly, I would probably walk out of here and forget about Him like I had in the past. So God did what needed to be done because He knows what is best for us. I was about to experience Him in an area I never had before, to know what it truly meant to fear God.

Again, I just tried to make a deal with God that if He would get me out of the trouble I had just gotten myself into, then I would do right by Him. It was a hurting heartfelt gesture on my part and I really meant it, but time and time again, I had said this kind of prayer, and once I had gotten out of the mess I was in then, I didn't keep my end of the bargain too well. But God was going to see to it personally that I would get on the right path and put more effort into keeping my end of the deal.

No sooner than I finished saying the words "God if you get me out of this mess I'm in, I promise I will do right by you," I heard this voice speak to me. It was as if someone was standing behind me and whispered into my right ear. It totally startled me and caused me to look around to see who said something, but I already knew I was in my cell alone so I said, "Whoa! What was that, God, are you speaking to me?" At this point in my life, I knew nothing about God speaking to people except the people of the Bible, but who was I that He would want to talk to me? I just thought He was out there in heaven just waiting to get people out of trouble when they needed Him really bad to help them.

I didn't know He was so real that He would actually talk to your average criminal like me. I was about to find out just how real and alive God really is. When I heard His voice, He only said one word, but one word from God can change a person's destiny, and boy, did it change mine. The one word was "Ecclesiastes," and when it startled me and I asked if He was talking to me, He said the exact same word again in that same whisper in my right ear…"Ecclesiastes."

Now remember I had already read through the Bible probably three times in my life before this incident happened, so I knew that Ecclesiastes was a book of the Bible, and I also had enough common sense to know that Satan or a demon would not in any way, shape, or form encourage me to read the Bible.

So I picked up my Bible and opened it to the book of Ecclesiastes, and I began to read from the beginning of chapter 1. I read through chapter 2, chapter 3, then

4, and now chapter 5; and all of a sudden, when I got to verses 4 and 5 of chapter 5, it was as if the words literally came alive and jumped off the pages of the Bible and shot straight into me and pierced my soul. What I read caused the realization that God had truly spoken to me and that we should not make empty promises to God. A fear fell over me that I knew I was now in the presence of a Holy God, and He was not interested in making deals with me. I felt as if God, at this very moment, could have punched my number, and I was in no position to enter the kingdom of heaven. It was "woe is me."

This awakening or revelation I just got, that God is real and very much alive, made me realize that here I was, a mere human, and I was about to be judged by a very powerful and awesome God, who created all things, and my life stood before him. I felt totally naked, and I did not want to be in this position very long at all. To tell you the truth, I was very much afraid to stand before Him. So much so that I couldn't literally stand before Him. This fear of God caused me to drop to my knees with my face to the floor and tears running down my face, begging for His forgiveness. It also caused me to get in agreement with Him and His Word real quick.

This was an act of true repentance, not just saying some "Jesus, come into my heart" prayer and then going on with business as usual. No, my whole life was about to take a different direction, because I now had a respect and a fear of God like I never had before. I now truly understood that only He and He alone holds the power to save your soul or to destroy it in hell fire. "And do not fear those who kill the body but cannot kill the soul. But rather fear Him who is able to destroy both soul and body in hell" (Matthew 10:28).

So the question is: what did I read to cause such a powerful reverence for God in my life? Let me remind you what I had prayed once again and then let's see what came alive to me and how God caused me to repent and get in agreement with Him and His Word.

My prayer was this: "Lord, if you get me out of this mess I'm in, I promise I will try to do right by you." God whispers "Ecclesiastes" in my ear. I read, "When you make a vow to God, do not delay to pay it; For He has no pleasure in fools. Pay what you have vowed, Better not to vow than to vow and not pay" (Ecclesiastes 5:4–5).

I was like a deer on a dark night caught in the headlights of an oncoming vehicle, nowhere to run because the light was shining on me. I thought God had just said I was a fool, but when I dropped to my knees with my face to the floor and tears streaming down my face, I said to God, "God, I know without a doubt you just spoke to me, with your voice and through your Word, and Lord, you are right, your Word is right, so whether you get me out of this mess or you don't get me out of this mess, I want to serve you. But I don't know how, you will have to teach me. I don't get it, God. I received Jesus into my heart and have been in and out of church all my life and even read the Bible a few times. I don't understand, what am I missing? I just don't get it."

I understood nothing about relationships or a relationship and communication with God Himself. I basically knew nothing about the Holy Spirit except that He was the third person of the God Head, but God Himself was about to teach me and deliver me in a big way, a way that only He could get the glory. When I broke down and lost my pride and told God He would have to teach me how to serve Him, He now had me in a place where He could shape and mold me into His image. A place of no more God adjust to me, because now I was teachable so God could adjust me to Him.

Since I knew for real that He had spoken to me once, I knew He could speak to me again. So I asked Him, "Now what? Where do we go from here?" He answered me with "First Corinthians." Well, I knew I had to go to 1 Corinthians and start reading, so God could show me what only He could show me, because my eyes were now being opened to the things of God and what He wanted me to see. Remember the blindness is taken off our hearts when we truly turn to Christ. "For it is God who commanded light to shine out of darkness, who has shone in our hearts to give the light of the knowledge of the glory of God in the face of Jesus Christ" (2 Corinthians 4:6).

I started reading in 1 Corinthians like the Lord told me to, and just like before, when I got to the place where God wanted to get something across to me, it jumped straight out of the Word and right into my spirit. It didn't take very long this time. I only had to read the first and second chapters. God was teaching me things all by Himself and I was excited.

This next thing He showed me was very important for every believer or anyone who reads the Bible. Here is what it is.

> But as it is written: Eye has not seen, nor ear heard, Nor have entered into the heart of man The things which God has prepared for those who love Him. But God has revealed them to us through His Spirit. For the Spirit searches all things, yes, the deep things of God. For what man knows the things of a man except the spirit of the man which is in him? Even so no one knows the things of God except the Spirit of God. Now we have received, not the spirit of the world, but the Spirit who is from God, that we might know the things that have been freely given to us by God. These things we also speak, not in words which man's wisdom teaches but which the Holy Spirit teaches, comparing spiritual things with spiritual. But the natural man does not receive the things of the Spirit of God, for they are foolishness to him; nor can he know them, because they are spiritually discerned.

> 1 Corinthians 2:9–14 (NKJV)

You see, when I got honest with God and told Him that He would have to teach me how to serve Him, I had no idea how that was going to happen, but God was clearly showing me how He does things. "By His

Spirit." I got out of these verses how ignorant we truly are when it comes to knowing and understanding God and His Word. That if we really wanted to know, then we had to learn to depend on the Holy Spirit, who is freely given to us by God to teach us all things and reveal the truth to us. He will lead us and guide us in all the things of God and reveal the Word to us. It is through the Holy Spirit that God opens up the Scriptures to us.

So now, I'm like "Wow! God, your Word says right here that by your Spirit you will teach me, so come on Holy Spirit and teach me, show me what I need to know." This became my lifeline, learning to depend on the Holy Spirit! Now I understand how I could read the Bible clean through from cover to cover three times before this and not get much out of it. I couldn't understand the Word apart from the Holy Spirit. Without the Spirit of God, it was just like reading any other book to me.

In the past I was proud when I said, "I am going to set myself to reading the Bible," so I could boast and brag about what I had accomplished. But it just doesn't work that way. God wants us to depend on Him and be connected to Him so that He can get the glory out of everything, even when it comes to reading and meditating in His Word. So now I knew if I wanted to learn how to live for and walk with God, I had to trust the Holy Spirit to show me how. I was hungry and He was feeding me. What would He serve me up next?

A PLATE OF HUMILITY

Now I was learning. I was excited about God teaching me by His Spirit, so I asked the question, "Where?" to the Holy Spirit. His reply, "Peter, not 1 Peter or 2 Peter, just Peter. So I went to 1 Peter and started reading. I didn't get anything until I got almost to the end of the book of 1 Peter, then chapter 5 verses 6 and 7 jumped out at me, only this time I had to really press into God for about two weeks before the revelation would come forth from what He was trying to tell me. Would I get frustrated and give up or keep seeking the Holy Spirit to bring forth what He was trying to tell me through these scriptures? "Therefore humble yourselves under the mighty hand of God, that He may exalt you in due time, casting all your care upon Him, for He cares for you" (1 Peter 5:6–7).

I understood the mighty hand of God because of the experience I had in that prison cell a few weeks before, but the "humble yourself" part I didn't get at all. Remember now, I was educated in the streets more than I was in school, and English had been my worst subject. I was in prison without easy access to a dictionary so I had no idea what "humble yourself" meant. Nor did I even think about asking anyone except my newfound friend, the Holy Spirit.

I was learning two things here. How to meditate in the Word until the answer came and to know and trust that He would give me the revelation to the questions I was asking.

Here I was chewing on these two scriptures for about two weeks, waking up in the morning, over and over in my mind, on my lips, "What are you trying to tell me, Lord?" Some things aren't going to come easy, but when you want the answers bad enough, He always comes through for you. I think sometimes He wants to see where your heart is at—if you are really serious about Him. Finally, the light came on as the Holy Spirit brought me the revelation. He gave it to me in a way I could clearly understand it.

He said to me, "What I am trying to tell you is this. Stop being so hardheaded and stubborn by trying to do things your way. Give me that mess of a life of yours, and I will show you how to do things my way. Humble yourself and learn from me." I got it, I finally got it. I had to lose my pride so God could work with me because our pride tells us that we don't need any help from anyone. It's that attitude that says I'll do what I want, when I want and how I want and because of that it leaves no room for anyone to teach us anything because we think we got it all figured out.

God was clearly showing me that I knew nothing at all about life the way He meant it to be. The next thing He said was, "I want you to forget everything you think you know and learn all things new from me." What God was doing with me was teaching me to trust Him and training me to hear His voice. I learned to cast all my cares on Him because if I was all focused on my situation, then I would not be able to seek Him out and His direction for my life.

I now had an understanding that God truly cared about me and my life was in His hands. He didn't want me sitting back and worrying if I was going to do twenty-five years behind bars. He had set me free from that, even though I was still locked up physically. The time or my surroundings didn't matter anymore. All that mattered was getting to know Him and His Word because the truth will make you free and that's what the Lord was doing. He was setting me free from the things of this world.

The more I let go of myself, the more He came in to instruct me. Where do you want me to go to next, Lord? "2 Timothy," so I went there. "Be diligent to present yourself approved to God, a worker who does not need to be ashamed, rightly dividing the word of truth" (2 Timothy 2:15). The old King James Version says, "Study to show yourself approved to God." This one was easy enough. Study to be seen and approved by God, not man. So I started spending more and more time in the Word than anything else. I was like a sponge soaking it up and God was pouring it out for me to soak up.

As I read the Bible daily, things would just jump out at me as God was delivering me and setting me free, and this was one of those things. "For do I now persuade men, or God? Or do I seek to please men? For if I still pleased men, I would not be a bondservant of Christ" (Galatians 1:10). When we learn to walk with

God, we should only seek out what is pleasing to Him and not fear what people think about us especially the ones who you used to run with.

The Bible says that people will think it strange because you no longer do the things you used to do and run with the crowd you used to run with. They will mock you and make fun of you, but that's all right because they will have to answer to God. "In regard to these, they think it strange that you do not run with them in the same flood of dissipation, speaking evil of you. They will give an account to Him who is ready to judge the living and the dead" (1 Peter 4:4).

The Word clearly tells us: "Therefore, Come out from among them And be separate, says the Lord. Do not touch what is unclean, And I will receive you. I will be a Father to you, And you shall be My sons and daughters, Says the LORD Almighty" (2 Corinthians 6:17–18)

When you learn to think for yourself and start separating yourself from the people you hung out with all your life because you choose to follow Christ, then they will speak evil of you and come against you, but the Bible warns us, "Yes, and all who desire to live godly in Christ Jesus will suffer persecution" (2 Timothy 3:12).

The Lord was warning me that this wasn't going to be an easy casual walk with Him. I was going to have to give up friends, people I had been close to all my life. They weren't going to like it, and some will come against me, but was I going to live my life to please myself and to please them, or was I going to let God be a Father to me and find out what is pleasing to

Him? I chose to find out what was pleasing to God and made a decision that I couldn't worry about what others thought of me. After all, they didn't die on the cross for me so that I could be saved and set free.

I decided to study to show myself approved unto God and that's what I set my mind and heart to doing. This was no easy task for me because I was in prison with a 1611 King James version of the Bible, and English was my worst subject ever. So to understand this old style of English was very hard for me, but I believe this was God's way to teach me how to always depend upon the Holy Spirit to reveal the Word to me.

One day as I was in the book of James, I read, "If any of you lack wisdom, let him ask of God, that giveth to all men liberally, and upbraideth not; and it shall be given him" (James 1:5 KJV). As soon as I read this, I said, "Lord, your Word says that if I lack wisdom, you will give it to me. Well, I lack the wisdom to understand this old English Bible, so please give me the wisdom to understand this so I can get to know you better. And He gave it to me, so much so that I now really enjoy reading and studying the King James Bible.

I do, however, since I am out of prison, study many different translations of the Bible now that I have the resources to do so to get a clear meaning of what God is saying to us through his Word.

But still in this prison cell, I was getting more and more understanding of the Word of God, and I'm seeing how the Word has to be the final authority that governs our lives. The Lord revealed to me, "For though we walk in the flesh, we do not war according to the flesh. For the weapons of our warfare are not carnal but mighty in God for pulling down strongholds, casting down arguments and every high thing that exalts itself against the knowledge of God, bringing every thought into captivity to the obedience of Christ" (2 Corinthians 10:3–5).

There is a war going on all around us, and we cannot fight spiritual beings with natural weapons. We need to dig deep into the Word and find out exactly what Christ did for us and who we are in Him. The biggest strongholds we need to pull down are in our mind and in the way we see things. Any thought that is not in line with the Word of God, we need to put that thought out of our mind and bring a thought from the Word of God into our mind to bring ourselves into a place of obedience to the thoughts of Christ or what the Word says about us.

Here are a couple of examples:

Example 1: "I don't see anything wrong with me doing drugs. I'm not bothering anyone or anybody. I don't see why they are illegal. They should let me just do what I want as long as I'm not hurting anyone." Now the knowledge of God says this: "It is not healthy for you to be a drunkard or a winebibber" or in my case a drug addict, and the Word tells us we should "obey all the laws of the land" as long as they are in agreement with God's Word. Now look at God's thoughts in the following scriptures because this is how we should be thinking.

Who has woe? Who has sorrow? Who has contentions? Who has complaints? Who has wounds without cause? Who has redness of eyes? Those who linger long at the wine, Those who go in search of mixed wine. Do not look on the wine when it is red, When it sparkles in the cup, When it swirls around smoothly; At the last it bites like a serpent, And stings like a viper. Your eyes will see strange things, And your heart will utter perverse things. Yes, you will be like one who lies down in the midst of the sea, Or like one who lies at the top of the mast, saying: They have struck me, but I was not hurt; They have beaten me, but I did not feel it. When shall I awake, that I may seek another drink?"

Proverbs 23:29–35 (NKJV)

And do not be drunk with wine, in which is dissipation; but be filled with the Spirit.

Ephesians 5:18 (NKJV)

Therefore g ird u p t he l oins o f y our m ind, b e sober, and rest your hope fully upon the grace that is to be brought to you at the revelation of Jesus Christ; as obedient children, not conforming yourselves to the former lusts, as in your ignorance; but as He who called you is holy, you also be holy in all your conduct, because it is written, Be holy, for I am holy.

1 Peter 1:13–16 (NKJV)

Example 2: "I don't know why God called me, I'm not worthy. I'm just an old sinner saved by grace, and I'm just hanging in there waiting to go to heaven, and it will all be better once I get there." Cast down that imagination and that kind of argument and bring your thoughts in line with what God says about you: I have been accepted in the beloved, and He has made me worthy because of the blood He shed on the cross for me. I have been made righteous and I am the righteousness of God in Christ Jesus, and I am more than a conqueror through him who loves me and I rule and reign with Him.

Having predestined us to adoption as sons by Jesus Christ to Himself, according to the good pleasure of His will, to the praise of the glory of His grace, by which He has made us accepted in the Beloved. In Him we have redemption through His blood, the forgiveness of sins, according to the riches of His grace.

Ephesians 1:5–7 (NKJV)

Now then, we are ambassadors for Christ, as though God were pleading through us: we implore you on Christ's behalf, be reconciled to God. For He made Him who knew no sin to be sin for us, that we might become the righteousness of God in Him

2 Corinthians 5:20–21 (NKJV)

Who shall separate us from the love of Christ? Shall tribulation, or distress, or persecution, or famine, or nakedness, or peril, or sword? As it is written: "For Your sake we are killed all day long; We are accounted as sheep for the slaughter. "Yet in all these things we are more than conquerors through Him who loved us. For I am persuaded that neither death nor life, nor angels nor principalities nor powers, nor things present nor things to come, nor height nor depth, nor any other created thing, shall be able to separate us from the love of God which is in Christ Jesus our Lord.

Romans 8:35–39 (NKJV)

I hope you are getting a picture of how this works because wrong thinking leads to wrong believing, and this leads to wrong things that come out of our mouths. What we fill our heart with, our mouth will speak, and what our mouth speaks, our actions will follow.

Now I was learning the ways of God and His kingdom and was being trained to recognize His voice and separate the wrong thoughts from His thoughts, and I was learning to discern what was of God and what wasn't of God. "For everyone who partakes only of milk is unskilled in the word of righteousness, for he is a babe. But solid food belongs to those who are of full age, that is, those who by reason of use have their senses exercised to discern both good and evil" (Hebrew 5:13–14).

I was starting to get off the milk and get in to the meat of the Word because the Lord God was doing a very quick work in me. I was hungry and He was feeding me and filling me up. "Blessed are those who hunger and thirst for righteousness, for they shall be filled" (Matthew 5:6).

I do want to point out that God speaks to us in many ways, and I could write a whole book just on that subject alone, but I am mainly focusing on His voice because to be led by His Spirit we need to know His voice, and we need to be able to discern His voice from that of the enemy. "My sheep hear My voice, and I know them, and they follow Me" (John 10:27) and "For as many as are led by the Spirit of God, these are sons of God" (Romans 8:14).

Anyway, as I was hearing Him more and more and communicating with Him more and more as the Holy Spirit was revealing truth to me, that question started to arise in me again about how I could have been almost pulled into hell by this demon even after I had accepted Christ.

After all, while I was in on my last parole violation, I had said the sinner's prayer and was going to church, reading my Bible. Surely, my place in heaven had to be secured, so how could this happen? God was about to give me a lesson in His Word that would forever tear down a stronghold in my thinking, and I pray that it will also be torn down in the body of Christ as well and in believers everywhere.

DECEIVED BY DOCTRINES
OF MEN

As I was seeking the Lord on this matter of how this could happen, "I don't understand Lord, what went wrong?" I thought I was saved, but where I was headed clearly showed me that I had been deceived into believing a lie. I had heard ministers and Christians tell me all my life that once you were saved, you would always be saved. This is a major stronghold in the lives of many believers today because it takes the message of grace and makes it into something that it is not.

The Bible clearly teaches that while we were yet sinners, Christ died for us so we can be dead to sin ruling and reigning in our flesh and be alive to God. Grace is the empowerment of the Holy Spirit working in our lives to overcome the sinful nature of our flesh. Grace is also God's unmerited favor toward us because we deserved eternal punishment, but God made a way out of that by sending His Son to take the punishment for us. The Bible also teaches that just because grace has been poured out doesn't mean we should take advantage of it and continue in our sins. When we have this wrong thinking that once we are saved, we will always be saved and don't worry about it if you mess up, just ask God to forgive you and He will. We use it as an excuse to never make the necessary changes to step into the fullness of God.

Yes, there is some truth to these things, but the greatest lies always contain the most truth. If we are told these two things all our lives but are never taught about true repentance, then we will never see our need to make the necessary changes to line up with God's Word. We will think no matter how much I keep sinning, God will forgive me, and besides, I know I'm saved because I accepted Jesus into my heart. Jesus calls this making the Word of God of none effect by taking the doctrines and commandments of men and teaching them instead of the truth of God's Word. "Hypocrites! Well did Isaiah prophesy about you, saying: These people draw near to Me with their mouth, And honor Me with their lips, But their heart is far from Me. And in vain they worship Me, Teaching as doctrines the commandments of men (Matthew 15:7–9).

Now let me show you how God tore down this wrong thinking in me. I want to show you by God's Word and how the Holy Spirit reveals truth. So I asked the Lord how could I be on my way to hell when I thought I should be saved? I heard the Holy Spirit say "Matthew 8."

I went there and started reading, and verses 5–13 caught my attention. This is an account of a Roman centurion who comes to Jesus for the healing of his servant, and Jesus was going to go and heal the servant, but the centurion understood the authority of the spoken Word and told Jesus just to speak the Word and it would be done. Now let's look at how Jesus replied to this.

> When Jesus heard it, he marveled, and said to them that followed, Verily I say unto you, I have not found so great faith, no, not in Israel. And I say unto you, That many shall come from the east and west, and shall sit down with Abraham, and Isaac, and Jacob, in the kingdom of heaven. But the children of the kingdom shall be cast out into outer darkness: there shall be weeping and gnashing of teeth.

> Matthew 8:10–12 (KJV)

Did you catch that? The children of the kingdom, not unbelievers, the children of the kingdom will be cast out into outer darkness, and there will be weeping and gnashing of teeth. This is what was happening to me the day I overdosed. The wall of blackness that appeared out of nowhere, now I understood it was the outer darkness and the terror I had experienced. I was crying and my teeth were chattering. God revealed the truth in His Word by His Spirit about what I saw and experienced in the natural realm here on earth.

So I questioned God further: "What do you mean the children of the kingdom will be cast out?"

This is what His reply was. In these scriptures Israel represented God's people at the time, which is a type of God's people today, which is us, the church. The Lord clearly took me to His Word when He said there are people who think they are of the kingdom of heaven, who read my Word but don't apply it, who show up in church to worship Him one day out of the week but forget about Him the rest of the week, people who honor Him with their lips but their hearts are far from Him. They are those who have a form of godliness but deny the power thereof, who profess to know God but their actions show otherwise.

> Therefore lay aside all filthiness and overflow of wickedness, and receive with meekness the implanted word, which is able to save your souls. But be doers of the word, and not hearers only, deceiving yourselves. For if anyone is a hearer of the word and not a doer, he is like a man observing his natural face in a mirror; for he observes himself, goes away, and immediately forgets what kind of man he was. But he who looks into the perfect law of liberty and continues in it, and is not a forgetful hearer but a doer of the work, this one will be blessed in what he does.

> James 1:21–25 (NKJV)

> He answered and said to them, "Well did Isaiah prophesy of you hypocrites, as it is written: 'This people honors Me with their lips, But their heart is far from Me.

> Mark 7:6 (NKJV)

Having a form of godliness, but denying the
power thereof: from such turn away.

2 Timothy 3:5(KJV)

God also said to me, "Where is your faith? Did you
not take heed to the warnings of disbelief and lack of
faith? You seek and believe only the blessings of my
Word, do you not also have faith to believe the curses
and consequences that will fall upon you if you do
not faithfully and diligently obey the Word of God?"
God doesn't honor part-time believers, believers who
think they are all right even though they are
actively and knowingly involved in sin.

Now understand this, the Lord was not talking
about us making mistakes because He surely has
enough mercy, grace, and love to cover our mistakes,
and besides, if anyone of us says we are without sin,
then we make God out to be a liar. We are spiritual
beings who live in a natural body, which is sinful flesh,
and the apostle Paul says in the book of Romans that
in our flesh dwells no good thing and that evil is just
as present in our everyday lives just as well as good
is, but only through Christ can we have the power to
overcome the evil.

What God was showing me here is that there are
people who know His Word and sit under His Word
constantly being taught or preached, but their hearts
are far from God and His Word. In other words, they
can go to every meeting in the world and do all the
right, good "Christian things" but never really give

God any thought or time of day. They know to do what God requires of them, which is fellowship with Him through the Holy Spirit and spending time with Him in His Word and applying it to their lives, but they don't do this. They just continue to do their own thing.

Jesus said, "If you love me, you will do what I command, and why do you call me Lord and not do what I say?" The book of James says to him who knows to do right but does not do it, to him it is sin. This is clearly talking about willfully sinning and willfully ignoring the promptings of the Holy Spirit.

When you are caught in this trap of the devil, the Bible says you are deceiving yourself because you are hearing the Word of faith being preached, but you are not grabbing a hold of it and making it first priority in your life. When we take the Word of God lightly and don't apply it, then we open ourselves up to deception and for different kinds of enemy spirits to be at work in us.

The Bible talks about a perversion of God's Word. It doesn't mean you are a pervert as the world sees a pervert. A perverse spirit puts a twist on God's Word to cause it to mean something different from what it is actually saying. And (Paul) said, "O full of all subtlety and all mischief, thou child of the devil, thou enemy of all righteousness, wilt thou not cease to pervert the right ways of the Lord?" (Acts 13:10 KJV). This spirit was at work in the Garden of Eden when the serpent put a twist on what God had commanded Adam. Eve was deceived into believing something different and something else than what God had truly said (Genesis chapter 3). This was very subtle deception on the part of Satan and it worked. It worked back then, and it is still at work today in the church through God's people. Satan is still putting a twist on God's Word to keep God's people in darkness and living a life of deception.

I hear so many Christians, when they make mistakes or they are just living in sin, use Romans 3:23 to justify their actions. They quote, "For all have sinned and come short of the glory of God." For those of us who are believers in Christ, this scripture is no longer an excuse for us. If you read the whole context of the scriptures around Romans 3:23, you will clearly see that apart from Christ, we all have sinned, and the whole earth is convicted and stands guilty before God, Jews, and Gentiles alike.

But now the righteousness of God is being made manifest in the face and person of Jesus Christ. What Paul is saying is that even though the Jews had the law of Moses, they still weren't justified in the eyes of God as being righteous and neither were the Gentiles who didn't have the law. Under the law, all the earth stands guilty before God, so we all have sinned and come short of His glory. These scriptures are all about the righteousness of God being made known to mankind, which is only by faith in Jesus Christ. And apart from Christ, we do fall short of God's glory. When we are in Him and His Word is abiding in us, we are no longer falling short of His glory. His glory is His presence and Holy Spirit in us.

Even the mystery which hath been hid from ages and from generations, but now is made manifest to his saints: To whom God would make known what is the riches of the glory of this mystery among the Gentiles; which is Christ in you, the hope of glory.

Colossians 1:26–27 (KJV)

Therefore being justified by faith, we have peace with God through our Lord Jesus Christ: By whom also we have access by faith into this grace wherein we stand, and rejoice in hope of the glory of God.

Romans 5:1–2 (KJV)

When we have accepted Christ and we yield to the Holy Spirit we are no longer falling short of the glory of God but the things of God and His kingdom are freely revealed to us because He lives inside of us.

For God, who commanded the light to shine out of darkness, hath shined in our hearts, to give the light of the knowledge of the glory of God in the face of Jesus Christ. But we have this treasure in earthen vessels, that the excellency of the power may be of God, and not of us.

2 Corinthians 4:6–7 (KJV)

These two scriptures sum it up: God made a way to plant Christ in our hearts, who is the glory of God Himself and to give us the knowledge of God's glory. So where is the glory contained? In us, God's earthen vessels. Now do you see we are no longer sinners falling short of God's glory? Through faith in Christ, we are justified and made righteous, and we are now containers of God's glory! This makes me want to shout and jump for joy!

But when we think wrong, we believe wrong, and the deception comes in and the enemy perverts the scriptures so you will use them to justify your wrong actions, so Romans 3:23 becomes an excuse and a stumbling block for you to continue in sin instead of repenting and pressing into the Holy Spirit so He can help you overcome and turn from the sin.

Here is another good example: I knew a guy who got delivered from being a homosexual. I was teaching him how to be a disciple of Christ, and God was using him mightily. We would walk the streets, pray for the sick and lame, and many souls were being saved. I was teaching him how to walk with Jesus and flow in the Holy Spirit, and it was awesome. But then God moved us to a different geographic location where there was a large population of the gay community. Now this guy had been free for about a year from this lifestyle. He knew the way to go, but he ended up being overtaken and fell back into the same trap and sin again.

It was revealed to me by the Lord what was going on with him, and I let him know that God was merciful and for him to repent, ask God's forgiveness and move forward. But he chose not to. He knew the difference between right and wrong, good and evil because he had been delivered and free, but he chose not to repent, because he had been told all his life that no matter what you do, just ask God to forgive you and He will, he saw no need to stop this particular sin, and it opened the door to deception and a perverse spirit.

One day he asked me where the scripture was that says "what the enemy meant for evil God would turn it around for his good." I said, "Why are you looking up that scripture?" He said, "Because of me sleeping with this other guy. Maybe God will turn it around for His good because I talk to my gay lover about Jesus." I said, "Dude, I don't think God will send you into someplace to sleep with another man to be a witness for Christ because it goes against His written Word."

Do you see how these spirits work to cause us to stumble at God's Word to justify our own sinful actions? Since then, my friend has repented and is serving the Lord once again, and the truth of the Word of God has made him free from sin and death. Just because we say a little prayer to receive Christ into our hearts, it doesn't make us a "real Christian." Yes, we do get saved that way, but that is only the beginning of our journey. We are to move forward in Him and His Word and grow up spiritually because the more truth we know, the more we will be set free and be able to overcome the desires of the flesh. But know this, the more you learn and the more you know, then the more you are held accountable to before God.

Christ desires to create His own image in us so we can rule and reign with Him and that's what makes us real Christians because we are becoming Christ-like. We cannot continue to straddle the fence because there are consequences. We can't serve God and have the ways of the world at the same time, and this is what I was doing. I thought I was saved. I knew the Word, heard the Word being preached, but was ruled by the devil. I wanted Jesus to be my savior but not my Lord. I didn't allow His Word to govern my life. When we have knowledge of the truth and turn from it, we are setting ourselves up for deception, judgment, and destruction. God said in His Word that He would never leave us nor forsake us, but He never said that we couldn't walk away from Him and forsake Him.

This is what the Word says about these things:

> For if we sin willfully after we have received the knowledge of the truth, there no longer remains a sacrifice for sins, but a certain fearful expectation of judgment, and fiery indignation which will devour the adversaries. Anyone who has rejected Moses' law dies without mercy on the testimony of two or three witnesses. Of how much worse punishment, do you suppose, will he be thought worthy who has trampled the Son of God underfoot, counted the blood of the covenant by which he was sanctified a common thing, and insulted the Spirit of grace? For we know Him who said, "Vengeance is Mine, I will repay," says the Lord. And again, "The LORD

will judge His people."It is a fearful thing to fall into the hands of the living God.

Hebrews 10:26–31 (NKJV)

Judgment begins with the house of God, and we need to be sure our feet are planted on a strong foundation of God's Word. We need to know the Word and put it into practice in our lives so we won't be deceived.

> For if, after they have escaped the pollutions of the world through the knowledge of the Lord and Savior Jesus Christ, they are again entangled in them and overcome, the latter end is worse for them than the beginning. For it would have been better for them not to have known the way of righteousness, than having known it, to turn from the holy commandment delivered to them. But it has happened to them according to the true proverb: "A dog returns to his own vomit," and, "a sow, having washed, to her wallowing in the mire."

2 Peter 2:20–22 (NKJV)

> These are wells without water, clouds that are carried with a tempest; to whom the mist of darkness is reserved for ever.

2 Peter 2:17 (KJV)

The outer darkness is where I was headed. But God was merciful not only to me by pulling me out, but to whoever is reading this, so He could reveal these truths and give these warnings to awaken His people up out of their slumber.

> And do this, knowing the time, that now it is high time to awake out of sleep; for now our salvation is nearer than when we first believed. The night is far spent, the day is at hand. Therefore let us cast off the works of darkness, and let us put on the armor of light. Let us walk properly, as in the day, not in revelry and drunkenness, not in lewdness and lust, not in strife and envy. But put on the Lord Jesus Christ, and make no provision for the flesh, to fulfill its lusts.

> Romans 13:11–14 (NKJV)

> So let's take heed to the instructions that James gives us: Therefore submit to God. Resist the devil and he will flee from you. Draw near to God and He will draw near to you. Cleanse your hands, you sinners; and purify your hearts, you double-minded.

> James 4:7–8 (NKJV)

The Bible says a double-minded man is unstable in all his ways. God was walking me through this, and now I had the answers as to why I was almost lost forever to the outer darkness. He was clearly showing me a foot in the kingdom and a foot in the world would never work. The double-mindedness was coming out of me as God was preparing to bring me out.

My Sheep Know My Voice

Through all of this, I was still facing twenty-five years with no parole, and I also had a parole violation to face on top of this. I was so wrapped up in the Lord Jesus Christ and His Word that nothing else really mattered to me. I had some awesome experiences with the presence of the Holy Spirit in my prison cell. One day, as I was getting ready to go outside to the courtyard, I felt this presence come in and literally wrap itself around me, and I experienced the tangible love of God the Father in a way like never before. I felt as if I was cradled in God's very hand itself, and what made this experience so much more different and more awesome than the others was that I was wide awake and enjoyed every second of it.

The book of James tells us to draw near to God and He will draw near to us. Oh, how true this is. God was really starting to speak to me in many different ways—through dreams and visions, through nature, and through other people. He gave me ears to hear and a heart to listen. I think the most amazing way He communicates with us is through His voice. I love hearing Him talk to me and interrupting my routine.

He was teaching and training me so I would know how to hear His voice and to depend on His voice and His counsel in every kind of circumstances that could come my way. Not only that but I believe our Heavenly Father just likes to have conversation with His creation. This is what I think He likes the most. God really enjoys our company, and we need to learn how to enjoy His company. You see I was only asking Him things concerning His Word and to reveal things to me in His Word, but He was trying to show me that He was concerned and interested in every area of our lives, and He wanted to be there in those areas as well.

So the Holy Spirit does what He does best. He gets me into the Word and leads me to the book of John chapter 10. A good part of this chapter is all about hearing His voice. When the Lord mentions the same thing in His Word about four or five times especially in the same chapter, it's a sure sign for us to really pay attention to what He is trying to tell us.

This verse really caught my attention: "My sheep hear my voice, and I know them, and they follow me" (John 10:27). I started meditating on this verse profusely. Over and over I would chew on it all day and all night. "My sheep hear My voice." His sheep follow his voice, and He knows them because of this. "All I want to do, Jesus, is hear your voice and follow your voice and to be led by your Spirit." Then one morning I awoke and heard "don't go outside today." I had this routine where I would get up and go out to the courtyard in the morning and get some physical exercise to keep in shape but not this particular morning. I thought, *this has to be His voice, so I'll just do what it said because maybe He wants me to spend some time with Him.*

So I stayed in and started to pray and was going to get into the Bible when not even ten minutes went by and they called my name over the intercom system to go up to see the dentist. I get up to the dentist, and they said they had tried to call me to come see them about two weeks earlier but I never came up. At this moment, I realized I wouldn't have heard them call me this time either, but it was God's voice that enabled me to hear them call me this day. "Don't go outside."

It was this intimate fellowship and training by the Holy Spirit of hearing His voice that would lead me straight up out of the mess I had gotten myself into. I was learning that God was interested in every area of my life, and it was important to hear and know His voice above all else. The Holy Spirit is our friend, helper, and our counselor, but if we don't practice the art of hearing His voice, how can we expect Him to counsel us, help us, lead us, and guide us?

There was this one day we were in a service in the prison chapel, and at the end of the service, before we went back to our cells, one of the guys started to have a heart attack. Everyone around him started to panic and yell about getting the medics, that he was going to die, but not the Christ in me. The Holy Spirit raised up a standard in me that caused me to go into action. I ran over to where this guy was sitting in his chair and pushed my way through the crowd of panicky people and told everyone to stop speaking death over this man and said, "Don't you know that life or death is in your tongue?" I then laid my hand on his chest and rebuked the spirit of death off him and thanked the Lord for totally healing him. Then the medics got there and rushed him away to the infirmary.

I had no idea what happened to this guy until the next day. I was out in the courtyard lifting weights when this same guy who had the heart attack came and found me to give me his testimony. He told me that he definitely had a heart attack, and he remembered how everyone around him was so fearful that he was going to die. Even he himself thought his time was up and he was going to die until I came over. He said the moment I laid my hand on him, he knew he was going to be fine because he felt power shoot straight into him from me. I told him it was the Lord Jesus who healed him, and he should give the glory and the praise to Him and Him alone.

The Lord was leading me by His voice and His Spirit, and He was about to bring me out of Egypt from under the hand of Pharaoh in a big way. I couldn't afford a regular attorney so the state appointed a public defender to defend my case. This lawyer just happened to be a new attorney, and I was his first major case. Any other time I had gotten myself into this kind of predicament and was facing major time, I would take whatever kind of deal the state would offer me, so I guess this is why they just appointed me this fresh guy to represent me. Evidently, they thought they had an open-and-shut case on their hands, and they could scare me into taking any deal they offered me just like in my previous court cases.

They were wrong this time because God was on my side. He taught me very well how to follow His lead and to hear His voice, to trust Him, and to let Him work on my behalf. God was my real attorney in this case, and I got the revelation that the court system no longer had any authority over me whatsoever except what the Lord allowed them to have. I understood I now belonged to Him and that my destiny was in His hands and not in the hands of the court system. The Lord had spoken to me and told me not to take any kind of plea bargain or any kind of deal they would try to offer me. I did as the Lord instructed.

The first time they came at me they said if I go to trial, they will see to it that I would get the maximum sentence of twenty-five years no parole, but if I would take a plea agreement and plead guilty, then they were willing to give me only fifteen years. Now, like I said, in the past I would have jumped on this deal to avoid the maximum sentence but not this time because I knew what God had said to me. Was I scared? Of course the fear was there trying to penetrate me and get me out of faith in what the Lord said, but I resisted the fear and chose to trust in what God had said to me so I told them no, no deal, I was willing to go to trial if I had to.

They said that I didn't know what was good for me, and they left frustrated because they thought that this was going to be an easy victory for them and another notch they could put in their belt of getting another so-called criminal off of the streets.

I guess about a month later, my lawyer comes back to see me again with another deal: this time ten years with the possibility of parole. I tell him no again, and then I get real bold with my faith and tell him that

I can't take any kind of deal because the Lord Jesus Christ told me not to. Well, needless to say, this guy thought I totally lost my mind. I explained to him how the police did an illegal search and I shouldn't have been charged with all these charges. I think this guy didn't really want to fight for me because he just wanted to be done with this case he found himself wrapped up in with a career criminal like myself. He just wasn't really sure if he could trust what I was telling him because of my past life and record. They already judged me guilty.

So my lawyer leaves that day, and I'm thinking I need to get rid of this lawyer and get a different one who will be willing to fight my case for me. The Lord kindly reminds me that He is fighting my case for me, and my job in this is to not look at how it seems to be, but to only trust in Him, and by the way, He tells me, "You won't be firing your lawyer." "All right, Lord, whatever you say," was my reply.

My lawyer comes back a third time and tells me that they are willing to give me the break of a lifetime. The court says if you plead guilty, they will only give you a five-year sentence, and you will be out in about three years. I said, "No, I can't take that chance because God is going to bring me up out of here. You just wait and see." Again my lawyer thought I was crazy, and he said, "Look, this is their final deal, and if you don't take it and you go to trial and you are found guilty, they will give you the twenty-five years, no parole." I said, "I can't take the deal because I know what God told me." He left and the State set a trial date.

From where I was in prison to the county they had to take me for trial was a few hours away, so they transported me there the day before my trial date. They put me in another prison overnight. In this other prison, I was in a cell alone with no Bible or anything else. I opened the locker door that was in this cell, and there were some pornographic pictures taped to the inside of the locker. It didn't matter that I took them down and ripped them up because one glance when I first opened that locker door was enough to plant an image in my mind and give place for the tempter to come in and torment me.

Satan came into that cell through the lust of the eyes, the lust of the flesh, and the pride of life, "For all that is in the world, the lust of the flesh, and the lust of the eyes, and the pride of life, is not of the Father, but is of the world" (1John 2:16).

I was about to go through a major spiritual battle that would last for about three hours. The enemy was trying to get me to give in to my sexual depravity by means of masturbation to satisfy my fleshly desires. He came in through the eye gate by causing me to accidentally look on those pictures and was trying to cause my flesh to sin because of the image that was planted in my mind. The pride of life says, "You can do things your way instead of God's way." Satan was also trying to get me out of faith and into fear by making me think I had made a big mistake by taking this case to trial, trying to make me think I wasn't worthy, there was no hope for me. The list of temptations and the list of lies goes on and on.

I didn't need a physical Bible in my possession because I was well armed with the sword of the Spirit, which is the Word of God itself. I had the Word of God alive and living inside of me, and every time the devil bombarded me with these thoughts, I hit him back with what the Word said. I cast down every imagination the enemy threw at me, and finally the breakthrough came.

The breakthrough came only because I submitted to God and His Word and resisted the devil and his thoughts. He had to flee from me because the Word says so. When the tempter left me, I literally felt about seven demonic spirits come out of my chest area and flee from that prison cell because they no longer had dominion over me. The blood of Christ defeated Satan at the cross, and we have the victory over the devil because of what Christ accomplished at Calvary.

> Blotting out the handwriting of ordinances that was against us, which was contrary to us, and took it out of the way, nailing it to his cross; And having spoiled principalities and powers, he made a shew of them openly, triumphing over them in it.
>
> Colossians 2:14–15 (KJV)

> And the seventy returned again with joy, saying, Lord, even the devils are subject unto us through thy name. And he said unto them, I beheld Satan as lightning fall from heaven. Behold, I give unto you power to tread on ser-

pents and scorpions, and over all the power of
the enemy: and nothing shall by any means hurt
you. Notwithstanding in this rejoice not, that the
spirits are subject unto you; but rather rejoice,
because your names are written in heaven.

Luke 10:17–20 (KJV)

I slept very good and peaceful that night, and I felt
so clean, pure, and refreshed. It was as if I had been
pressure-washed from the inside out, cleansed by the
blood of Christ and the Word of God. I awoke nice
and early and had my breakfast and off to court I went.
The devil still wasn't ready to let me go without a fight.

They present my case before a trial judge, not a
jury, so this judge gets to hear my case and make his
judgment over the matter. The first thing that goes
wrong for the State is that the girl who was to testify
against me didn't show up for court. They needed her
testimony to say the drugs that were found in her house
were mine. Since she didn't show up, all they had were
the police reports. So they read the police reports and
proceeded to prosecute me anyway.

My lawyer surprised me and did a really good job of
proving illegal search and all that. He really fought on
my behalf. My sisters were in the courtroom, expecting
me to walk out of there that day, but like I said, the
enemy wasn't going to let me go without a fight. Even
though my lawyer proved me innocent, the judge
still found me guilty, but he only gave me one year.
Hallelujah, Jesus, only one year! I was happy because I

had five months in already, and I would be home in no time, right? Wrong, because once I got my paperwork, I saw that it was one year in the county jail, and that time wouldn't start until after I had my parole hearing, which meant that I would have to go back to county jail, which I didn't want to do. But all this was working together for my good because God was on my case.

I got back to my prison, and the Lord says to appeal it. I told my lawyer I wanted to appeal. He said, "Are you nuts? They will take you to Circuit Court and give you a whole new trial, and you will be facing the twenty-five years all over again." I told him that God had told me to appeal the sentence because it was not His will for me to go to the county jail and do a whole year after I left this place. My lawyer said, "No problem," because he now knew I had God on my side and I was letting God direct my steps. In the meantime, this helped me out because now that I was sentenced, I could see the parole board over my parole violation. They saw on paper that I had to go to county jail to do a whole year, so they reinstated my parole to get me out of their system, or so they thought.

Once my lawyer filed the appeal papers, the county jail couldn't take me because it was as if I never had been sentenced and was still awaiting trial. This way I was able to stay in the prison system where I was and continue growing in the Lord. I joined the choir in the prison chapel, and then the Lord promoted me to the prison ministry team because they have it set up just like the Word says. The church is the church whether you are a part of the Body of Christ behind bars or out here in the free world. Freedom has nothing to do with your location. It has all to do with the condition of your heart and soul through your relationship with God. There are more people locked up in the prison of their minds than in physical prisons. The only way to be truly free is through the blood of Christ and the Word of God because it is the truth that makes you free from the things of this world.

Now God had me doing more and more ministry in the prison. I started preaching the Word by the power of the Holy Spirit, laying hands on the sick more and more, and seeing God move miraculously, and all before I was baptized in the Holy Spirit. That would come to pass a few years later.

Anyway, God was using me for His glory behind prison walls. He started telling me that I was going to take the gospel of the kingdom around the world and heal the sick. So I knew for sure that He was bringing me up and out of where I was. I was getting ready to be set before my greatest challenge yet. The preaching in prison was just preparing me for what God had planned for me next. My day in court finally arrived again, and it didn't look good in the natural. I was going back in front of the same judge who had sentenced me back in 1999 to the fifteen years all suspended but eight on my second major felony.

I still trusted the Lord. Everyone in the holding cell with me that day was worried about their cases, but they noticed I was not. I started giving testimony about the goodness of the Lord and sharing the gospel with them. These hardened criminals were giving their hearts to the Lord as the presence of the Holy Spirit was shining light into the darkness and the Lord Jesus Christ was bringing a renewed hope to them. We had a revival in that cell as I prayed for those men and asked the Lord to bless them, and He did. One by one they went to have their cases heard, and one by one the Lord had mercy on them. They all came back with good reports, and some of them didn't come back at all because they were released on the spot.

Then it came time for my case to be heard. I was back in that holding cell thanking God and praising Him for what He was about to do in this courtroom to glorify Himself. I had prayed, "Lord, let them make a decision here today that would leave them scratching their heads." God answered in a big way and did just that. I didn't even have to have a trial. The state presented a deal to the defense and we accepted it, and the judge went along with it. The judge literally started scratching his head as he looked at me and said, "Mr. Nalley, I have no idea why I am about to make the decision I am going to make here today, seeing as how you appeared before me a few years back and I gave you fifteen years that time with a suspended sentence of seven years. By all rights I could revoke your probation, but that I am not going to, and not only that, the state has agreed to have you plead guilty to one possession charge and they will throw out the rest, and we all have come into agreement to sentence you to one year and one day to the division of corrections to run concurrent with any other sentence you might be serving, no new probation or anything.

This meant that my new sentence would run with what I was already serving, and since they reinstated my parole already on that sentence, I only had to finish out this one-year sentence. This meant that I would be out in a few more months.

God wasn't finished in the courtroom because after the judge handed down my sentence, he asked me if I had anything I wanted to say on my behalf and I said, "Yes, as a matter of fact, I do have something I need to say." As I went to stand up, my lawyer grabbed me by my arm, and said, "You don't have to say anything. You have already been sentenced." I don't know what my lawyer thought I was going to say. Maybe he thought I was going to say something about the injustice of the criminal justice system or something along those lines, but the Lord didn't have me there for that.

He had me positioned before kings and governors, in this case judges and law enforcement officers, and the Holy Spirit was jumping and kicking in me like a baby. I was pregnant with a message that needed to come out. Oh yes, the spirit of fear was there, trying to stop me from opening my mouth, but I had to obey the Master who was my true Judge.

The first thing that I said was "I want to thank you, Your Honor, for the sentence you gave me here today. I want to let you know you didn't make a mistake because, while I was incarcerated this time, I had yielded my life to Jesus Christ, and I know you won't ever see me in your courtroom again. Also, Your Honor, it doesn't matter that you hold a high position in this court and live by the laws of the land, and you police officers, it doesn't matter that you have a good job and put people like me behind bars, and everyone else in this courtroom, it doesn't matter if you never have been in trouble like I have been. In the eyes of God, there is no difference between us, and according to the laws of God, we are all convicted of sin. We all stand guilty before God, and unless we receive Jesus Christ as our Lord and Savior, we are all condemned to eternal damnation. The Bible says all of us have sinned and come short of His glory, and the wages of our sin is death, eternal punishment. But the gift of God is eternal life through our Lord and Savior, and whoever calls on the name of the Lord will be saved. The only difference between you and me is that my sins are out in the open where all can see, and unless you call on Jesus Christ, you will not be forgiven of your sins."

The whole courtroom was in silence as God gave me His platform to share His gospel. Everyone in the place was stunned that I preached to the judge and the police officers. The judge looked at me and said, "Mr. Nalley, I hope your commitment to Christ is real because I have seen many people go to jail and get jailhouse religion, but I really do pray I never see you again! Court dismissed!"

THE DESIRES OF YOUR HEART

What a day in court, what a victory, and all because I chose to have faith in God. It was because of Him and Him alone that I came out of that courtroom with only a one-year sentence that was running concurrent with my previous sentence, so after I do a couple more months, then I'll be out. Even though I didn't get any probation on this new sentence, I would still have about thirteen months of parole to do on my old sentence after my release. But that seemed like a small thing to me after what I had just won a victory over. This all happened because I had learned to trust in the Lord with all my heart and not lean on my own understanding, to sit and commune with Him and get His direction for everything. I had learned that I belong to Him and that He had good plans for me, and nothing could happen to me unless He allowed it to. I was safe in His arms as long as I walked with Him.

When I got back to the prison where I was doing my time, I was walking down the sidewalk to my housing unit when another one of my friends, who was a believer, yelled out the window to me and he said "Hey, Donald, you still made out real good because I was praying for you and the Lord told me He was going to give you a year so what did you get?" I said,

"A year, but it is now running concurrent instead of consecutive and I get to finish it out here, but since I already have eight months in, I'll go home in about two more months." Then my friend said, "The Lord also showed me that He gave you this time because He isn't finished preparing you for what He has called you to do." I was happy and praising God for His goodness.

I spent my time digging more and more into the Word of God. I was learning about the gifts of the Holy Spirit in 1st Corinthians chapter 12. After that I was reading in the book of Matthew when this stood out to me: "But seek ye first the kingdom of God, and his righteousness; and all these things shall be added unto you" (Matthew 6:33, KJV).

I know in the context of Matthew 6:33. It's talking about if we seek the kingdom of God first above everything else, then all the other natural things would be added, but I got a revelation from the Lord that if I just seek Him, to get to know Him and draw close to Him, then all these spiritual gifts would also follow and they did. I just opened myself up to however God wanted to use me. I am His vessel and am here just to do what is pleasing to the Father. I started preaching the Word more and more to all those around me, giving God praise and glory in everything. It didn't matter that I was in prison. All that mattered was hanging out with Christ and communing with the Holy Spirit.

God was using me to set people free, and I was finally finding my purpose in life. It was to lay it all down and live for Him. I still had a way to go yet because I still wasn't quite dead to myself. There were a few things I had to overcome, which would still cause me to stumble in the near future, but for now, I was pressing in. The time flew by fast, and it was getting close to my release date. I was due to get out about a week before Christmas. God's timing was awesome. I would be home for Christmas for the first time in a long time. As usual, I would go back and move in with my sister because she always seemed to have a place in her heart for me and a spare room to put me.

I was ready to get out of here and move on with my life. I didn't know how I was going to act around my family with my newfound zeal for Christ because they weren't godly church-going people. But that is where I had to go to live. My sister doesn't do drugs or anything like that, but other people in my family are a different story. All the people that I've known and grown up with and work construction with got high, but I thought I would be strong enough to be around them. I didn't really give it much thought at all to tell you the truth. I was just happy to be getting out. Right before I got out, I was thinking about my daughter, who I had not seen for fifteen years. She would be twenty-one years old now. I never stopped thinking about her and I never stopped loving her. I had no idea where she was or even if she ever thought about me, but one thing I did know was my loving God and Father was on my side, and if anyone could make something happen, it would be Him.

I knew the Word had a promise for me so I opened my Bible, and I found it in the book of Psalms. "Delight yourself also in the LORD, And He shall give you the desires of your heart. Commit your way to the LORD, Trust also in Him, And He shall bring it to pass" (Psalms 37:4–5). Then I prayed, "Lord, your Word says right here that if I delight myself in you then you will give me the desires of my heart. My greatest desire is to meet my daughter. I don't know where she is, but you do. I've been delighting myself in you, so I trust you will bring this to pass. Thank you, Lord Jesus, for hearing me and answering me." I finished praying and then went on about my business. Because I cast this care on Him, it was no longer weighing me down. It was now up to the Lord to make it happen.

My day came for release. It was December of 2005 and I would be home for Christmas, and it was a wonderful Christmas because this is the time of year that all your family will come by for visits, and I got to see most of my family over this Christmas season. One thing I lacked though was the fellowship that I had with all my brothers in Christ in the prison. I had certain brothers that were as passionate about the Lord as I was, so I hung out with them throughout the day in the prison, and all we talked about was the Lord and the Word of God, but now I didn't have that, and my family weren't exactly believers. Some were, but talking about Christ wasn't their cup of tea.

I didn't understand the importance of getting involved in a local church and meeting other believers. Sure, in prison we hung out together because we were also caged in together, and like I said, I still wasn't quite dead to myself, so I still had a fear of what regular church folk would think about someone like me that was just getting out of prison.

This would be one mistake I would learn from in the near future and wouldn't make twice. I thought I could walk with Christ and hang out with my same old crowd of people. We either have an influence over them, or they will have an influence over us. I didn't fully understand yet that what you look at, what you put in your ears, and even things you can smell, can all cause your flesh to crave things. For now I was enjoying my holiday season with my family, and it was about to even get better as once again God would do a miracle.

It was New Year's Eve 2005, and I was sitting in my sister's living room watching television when my sister came in and handed me a letter. She said, "Here, you have a letter from someone in Michigan." I said, "I don't know anyone in Michigan unless it is one of those ministries I was writing to while I was in prison, but wait a minute, the prison doesn't forward your mail, and besides, I didn't recall a ministry in Michigan."

As soon as I looked at the return address on the letter, tears started streaming down my face. I knew God had answered my prayer. The first name was the same, but the last name was different. I said to my sister, "This letter is from my daughter." She said, "How do you know? You haven't even opened it up yet." I said, "I know because I prayed and asked God to bring her into my life, and I know this is the answer to my prayer." So I opened the letter and started to read, and sure enough, it was from my daughter. She was looking for me and her brother. She wasn't sure if she even had the right address because it was the only address she had to link her to Maryland.

She told me how she had gotten adopted at the age of thirteen in Arizona and how she had gotten to pick the family that she wanted to live with. It was a Christian family. When she turned eighteen, they gave her all the paperwork that they had from her past life, and she found this address of my sisters and wrote not knowing that my sister owned her home and had lived there over twenty years at the time this happened. I started praising God for what only He could do, and of course, Satan was there trying to discredit the work of the Lord. My nephew said, "God didn't have anything to do with it. She had the address and just decided to write." I said, "Well, tell me how come she didn't write three years ago when she turned eighteen and first got the file on herself, but as soon as I prayed in faith I got a letter from her two weeks later?" He didn't know how to answer that. I said, "You can think what you want to think, but I know this was God who did this," and I went on thanking and praising the Lord for what He had done.

I wrote back to my daughter to let her know she had found me. So she wouldn't think I was some kind of a predator just trying to lure her in, I made sure I sent copies of her birth certificate and baby footprints and some pictures of her when she was a little girl. We started building a relationship, and two months later, she came for a visit to Maryland to meet me and the rest of her natural family. God is good!

If you are reading this and you have children out there somewhere who you think may not want anything to do with you, don't ever lose hope because when God is on your side, all things are possible. Put your situation in God's hands and wait on Him to do what he does best. He is the restorer of the breech. I got to meet my daughter because God gave me the desire of my heart, and He will do that for you too, but you have to trust Him and give Him room to work. He is moved by your faith in Him, which says "only He can do this." This is a very important characteristic of faith. Don't be moved by what you see, feel, or think. Only be moved by the promises and conditions He laid out in His Word!

My daughter visited for two weeks, and we continue to keep in touch to this very day, slowly building our relationship and getting to know one another. Now the Lord would have to work on my son because he grew up thinking I was a deadbeat dad, which I was, and I can't blame him for feeling this way, but God has a plan for that situation also which will come much later. My daughter headed back to Michigan with a lot of answers to the questions she had always had, and I thank the Lord for all He has done!

I was so happy and standing tall. I'm out of jail and enjoying life, but I was skating on thin ice. I had gone back to work building houses with my nephew, and being around the same bunch of guys while they were getting high didn't help me at all. Even though all those demons had come out of me in that prison cell, I still had one last strong man to battle who was determined to take me out with a vengeance.

A ROCKY ROAD:
THE FIGHT OF MY LIFE

I don't know how it happened or when it started, but it just did. Somehow I slipped and slid back into casual drug use. I thought a little here and there on the weekends wouldn't hurt me, and if I was real careful, I would be able to get around the timetable of when I had to give urine samples for parole and probation. Well, it started out that way, but it sure didn't finish up that way. I was able to beat the system for a while, but things always catch up to you in the long run. You might be asking, how can a guy like me who has had such awesome experiences with God and also who's had stern warnings from God fall back into the same trap of the enemy again?

Well, Satan is very cunning and deceiving. I got out of prison thinking I was going to save the world, but I didn't see the importance of getting involved with a local church and connecting with other believers. I thought it was me and Jesus up against the world, and I had it all together. The Bible says pride comes before a fall. "Pride goes before destruction, and a haughty spirit before a fall" (Proverbs 16:18). "Therefore let him who thinks he stands take heed lest he fall" (1 Corinthians

10:12). I was full of pride and didn't even realize it. It was pride that was telling me "You can do this and get away with it," "Just one time won't hurt," "You can outsmart the system because you only have a year of parole left to do." Pride always says, "I got this figured out, and I don't need help from anyone. I'm going to do this my way." I've learned the hard way that my way doesn't work. Only God's ways work.

I started out just using a little cocaine here and there, and then it led me back to doing a little heroin here and there until I injured myself one day at work. I was moving a sheet of ¾-inch plywood, which I had done thousands of times and also I think from all the heavy work we did my stomach muscles were already weakened so I must have twisted wrong or stretched myself too far, but I felt something tear in my lower stomach. I would find out later that it was a double hernia, one on the left and one on the right. So I went to see a doctor, and they put me off from work until I could have surgery to fix these hernias. Since it was an injury at work, I would get paid while I was off work, and they would pay for my surgery. I also had a legitimate excuse for the parole board why I didn't have to work. It seemed as if everything was going in a good direction for me because, now that I was hurt and laid up, I couldn't run as much to get the illegal drugs I desired so I thought this may be God's way to get me off of the drugs.

One thing I failed to realize was that God would not harm a person to try to teach them something. I got hurt in the first place because I got drawn away from God because of my own lust and desires and cravings of the flesh.

> Blessed is the man who endures temptation; for when he has been approved, he will receive the crown of life which the Lord has promised to those who love Him. Let no one say when he is tempted, "I am tempted by God"; for God cannot be tempted by evil, nor does He Himself tempt anyone. But each one is tempted when he is drawn away by his own desires and enticed. Then, when desire has conceived, it gives birth to sin; and sin, when it is full-grown, brings forth death. Do not be deceived, my beloved brethren. Every good gift and every perfect gift is from above, and comes down from the Father of lights, with whom there is no variation or shadow of turning.

> James 1:12–17 (NKJV)

Being hurt is not a perfect gift from above.

Anyway I kind of thought I was getting off these drugs, but the doctor prescribed me oxycodone. This made me think I didn't need these other illegal drugs. I could just do these pills the doctor gave me and the parole people won't be able to do anything about this because these are prescribed to me by a doctor. I told you the enemy is very cunning. You don't give a recovering heroin addict oxycodone because it gives you almost the same high as the heroin itself, and this strongman was at work in me, slowly establishing his rule over my flesh again. Now I had a major problem. The oxycodone caused my flesh to crave the heroin in a big way. So I went looking up my old shoplifting friends, and sure enough, they were still doing the same old thing.

I had my heroin connection again, and I got hooked worse than before. I was shooting up every day and couldn't go without it. I started to get dirty urine results at parole again because I couldn't control my habit anymore. I again became a slave to the drug and the pills. I was playing this "poor, helpless old me" routine in front of people like I was always in pain from the hernias, but the truth was, I was so high all the time and numb that I didn't really feel any of it until I started to come down off the drugs. Then one more fix would just numb me out all over again. I just had this thing down to a tee of making people think I was so hurt and sick so they would pity me. I had this down so good that I even fooled the parole violator guy who came to pick me up for another parole violation. I violated again because of dirty urine. They couldn't get me for not reporting because I kept reporting even though I knew I was dirty. I was just so foolish to think they wouldn't test me for other drugs because I was on prescription medications.

Here is what happened. The doctor scheduled me for my first operation for my hernia on the left side. I went through the surgery and then went home to my sister's house. I was laid up in my bed about two weeks later because I was still pretty sore from the surgery. A man came to arrest me for parole violation, and I put on such an act that I couldn't hardly walk and was in so much pain that this guy didn't arrest me because he was afraid I would hurt myself all over again. So he made me promise that once I healed up good enough, I would come and turn myself in. Of course I had no intention of turning myself in, but if this would keep me out of jail for the moment, then what would a little lie hurt?

I went back down to my room and asked the Lord to forgive me. This time in the midst of my mess at least I didn't forget about God completely. I was still looking to Him for help. I realized that I was straying off His path for me, so I started crying out for Him to help me. Day and night I was calling out to Him because I knew I couldn't stop the heroin without supernatural intervention from God.

When I was able to really move around again I didn't turn myself in, but God was going to see to it that my word would be upheld. The first chance that I got I went and picked up my friends, and off we went on one of our journeys to Baltimore to sell stolen goods and buy drugs. We got some heroin and were shooting up in the middle of traffic when the cops surrounded us. They were doing routine license plate checks for stolen cars, and when they ran my plate through their in-car computer, it came back that the owner of the vehicle was a parole violator, which of course, was me.

At least I didn't have far to go to the division of corrections headquarters since I was already in Baltimore. God spared me and had mercy on me because after a good night's sleep, I awoke in the morning and had no withdrawal symptoms from the drug use, and the desire and cravings for the drugs were gone. The enemy was mad and he would lash back in a big way and try to kill me and make me lose all hope of a future, but God, who knows all things, would prepare me for the battle before it even came. Coming back to prison this time would prove to be the best thing to happen to me. In man's eyes going to jail isn't a good thing, but because my heart was still with God through this whole relapse and backsliding episode, it was an answer to my cry for help from the Lord.

This is why we shouldn't judge people by what is going on in their lives because we as people tend to look at the appearance of things, but God is looking at the person's heart, and my heart was still with God even though I had fallen backward.

Now that I was sober-minded and thinking clearly, I got right back into the Word of God and started seeking Him again. Not only that, I came across a Christian magazine with faith-filled testimonies from a well-known ministry in Fort Worth, Texas. I enjoyed the teachings so much in this magazine that I wrote to their ministry, and they sent me a few books that really helped me deepen my relationship with the Lord and understand the importance of how faith is produced in you by planting the Word in your heart in abundance. I was getting a clear revelation that faith works by believing only what God says, getting in agreement with Him and confessing it out of your mouth and calling those things that be not as if they were. I learned not to look at the circumstances or how we feel but only to God and His Word. All the books I ever read from this ministry always pointed me to Christ and His Word. I read one of their books about healing, how we take healing by faith for our bodies and how to walk in diving health because Jesus paid the price for not only the salvation of our soul but also the healing of our body.

Like I said, God knew ahead of time the battle I was about to go through, and looking back, I can clearly see why He connected me with this teaching ministry.

If you need brakes for your car, you don't go to a grocery store to get them. Likewise, if you want to learn how to live by faith, then you learn from people who have been doing it for a long time. I didn't know anything about this ministry, but God knew them very well, and He knew how to connect me with their teachings, which would prove to be the very thing that would save my life. Through their teachings I learned how to have a correct foundation in God and His Word in the area of faith. It was God at work through a ministry in Texas to reach me, an inmate in a prison in Maryland. What exactly was God preparing me for? It surely wasn't anything to do with my parole because I had only six months left total on my sentence, and all they did was send me to a drug rehab prison for a few months.

God prepared me to go into a battle with the full armor of God on. He had me dressed for battle, but was I ready? Would it be a victorious battle, or would I be defeated by the onslaught of Satan?

I started to get sick one day, itching all over like something was crawling under my skin. I didn't know what it was, and then everything about me turned yellow. My skin, my eyes, my urine, my feces—everything was as yellow as a caution sign. I couldn't really hold any food in my system, and I had diarrhea all the time. My stomach was all messed up, doing flip-flops. I had profuse head pain, and to top it all off, I was in prison, so getting medical help isn't like you can call 911 and have an ambulance come. I had to put in a medical slip and wait a few days to see a doctor. Meanwhile I was in terrible shape. In the natural this is what we have been trained to do. You get sick, you go see a doctor. But all this was about to forever change with me because the diagnosis I was about to get would prove to be fatal. I believe it went this far so I would know and understand the true power of the resurrection of Jesus Christ. That power was about to raise me from the grips of death a third time.

When I went to see the doctor, they ran some tests on me, blood tests and other things, and I was diagnosed with hepatitis C. The doctor told me that I had acute hepatitis C, and that it was the worst case he had ever seen, that my liver was totally shot, and there was no hope for me. He gave me six months at the most to live, but said that I would be lucky if I lived passed six weeks. He gave me a written report on paper of the diagnosis and basically said I was going to die, and there was nothing they could do for me.

The Word of God says, "When the enemy shall come in like a flood, the Spirit of the Lord shall lift up a standard against him" (Isaiah 59:19). The Holy Spirit was about to lift up a standard against this enemy of sickness that was coming against my body, and all the studying, meditation, and preparation the Lord had me doing concerning healing and the finished work that Christ did at the cross was about to pay off in a big way. The Bible tells us that out of the abundance of the heart, your mouth will speak, and what you put into your heart from the Word of God the Holy Spirit will bring to your remembrance.

When the doctor said, "You are going to die and there is nothing we can do for you," I looked him straight in the eye and said to him, "You don't know Jesus Christ, do you? He is my Savior, my Redeemer, and my Healer. It doesn't matter what you say or what this medical report says. It only matters what the Word of God says, and the Word of the Lord says He bore my sicknesses, He took my diseases. The chastisement for my peace was upon him, and by His stripes, I am healed, and what that means is this: He took this disease that is in my body and nailed it to the cross over two thousand years ago. So the healing has to manifest itself in my body, just you wait and see! Jesus is going to heal me" (see Isaiah 53).

Well, needless to say, the doctor looked at me as if I had lost my mind, but when you read what I was quoting from Isaiah 53, the chapter starts out with the most remarkable statement that should set the standard for all believers. "Who hath believed our report? And to whom is the arm of the Lord revealed?" (Isaiah 53:1, KJV). I had two choices set before me that day. Which report would I believe: the medical report or the report of the Lord? If I had believed the medical report, then the arm of the Lord would not have been revealed to me, and I would not be revising this book 11 years later. Jesus said many times to many different people, "Let it be done to you according to your faith" or according to what you truly believe. The fact of the matter is this: to the doctor, his truth was that I was going to die. The condition of my body and the symptoms of sickness said the same thing, but this is why you cannot go by how you feel or what you see. These things were not "truth," they were only facts. I only looked at what God said in His Word, which is "truth," and His truth was alive in my heart and that was the only thing I chose to believe.

Now, was this an easy battle to overcome? I would be lying if I told you that it was. After the doctor diagnosed me with this fatal disease, they had me quarantined down in a medical cell because this stuff was highly contagious. The prison was a very old prison, so when they put me in this cell down in the basement, I felt like Paul and Silas being locked up in the inner prison. While I was locked up down there, I was separated away from everyone. I was alone but glory to God I had my Bible.

I went through a major battle with the enemy. He kept tempting me to look at my condition and think about what the doctor said to try to get me to doubt God's Word. If Satan could get you to come in agreement with his lies and confess them out of your mouth, then he will win the battle. I left no place for this and gave it my all to pay him no mind.

I just kept pressing into God's Word more and more to keep the faith alive and active in my heart. I learned that when we are consistent in our meditation of His Word, this is where the power of faith is produced. So when we are consistent in diligently seeking God through His Word, then His power will manifest in our lives because He is a "rewarder to those who diligently seek Him" (Hebrews 11:6).

I believed in my heart the report of the Lord so I knew healing had to manifest itself in my body. I believed nothing else. I gave no place to the devil. I ministered to the inmates on the food detail, who brought my meals by to feed me. I also witnessed to the guards who were with them. I prayed for them, led them to the Lord, and blessed them.

Day by day, as I feasted on God's Word and fed it to all those who would pass by my cell, my body was getting stronger and stronger. My health was coming back into my body. God's Word is a medicine to all who will believe. "My son, give attention to my words; Incline your ear to my sayings. Do not let them depart from your eyes; Keep them in the midst of your heart; For they are life to those who find them, And health to all their flesh" (Proverbs 4:20–22).

Meditation in God's Word was bringing life back into my spirit and producing health to my body. I was taking no other medicine because according to the doctor, there was no hope for me. So they did nothing but waited for me to die. Then one day, I awoke in the morning, a month or more had passed after they quarantined me, and I knew that I knew I was totally healed and whole. So I started to demand that they take me back up to see the doctor so that he could check me out again. The doctor did all the same tests on me because he couldn't believe how healthy I looked. The medical report came back, and they found no trace of the hepatitis C in my body whatsoever.

The doctor looked at me and said, "I don't understand it. This first report says you are going to die and your liver is deteriorated. But now this new report shows none of that, and as a matter of fact you are the healthiest person I have examined in a while." I looked at him and said, "I told you Jesus Christ is my healer and all the glory goes to Him." I went all the way back to my cell, rejoicing and praising the Lord.

Then the Lord revealed to me in the Word the warning He gave to the man at the pool of Bethesda after Jesus healed him. We find this stern warning: "Afterward Jesus found him in the temple, and said to him, "See, you have been made well. Sin no more, lest a worse thing come upon you" (John 5:14). I know what the Lord was saying to me. Don't fall into the same sin anymore. Stay off the drugs or a worse thing can and will come upon you.

Redeemed and Free

Shortly after I was totally healed and made whole I got released. It was December 17, 2006. Before I got out, I diligently sought the Lord as to where He wanted me to go to church. I now understood how important it is to get around other believers. The Lord led me to a church where they welcomed me with open arms. I became a part of this fellowship and was actively involved in serving with the gifts God had given me. The more I humbled myself to the leading and guiding of the Holy Spirit, the more the Lord would use me for His service and exalt me. I started to really flow in the gifts of healing and was seeing God do some awesome things. I had extreme faith for healing especially after witnessing what God had done first hand in my own life.

The Lord wasn't finished with me yet as He would continue to strengthen my faith. Now I had to go back to my workman's compensation physician and get this other hernia fixed. It was a lot different this time because before I went down for surgery, the hospital chaplain came to visit and give me some encouraging words from the Bible, but I don't know who encouraged who the most, me or her. The surgery was a big success, and of course the doctor prescribed oxycodone to me once again for the pain. Now I had a choice to make: would I take these narcotics and run the risk of full-blown addiction again, or would I close the door on this spirit and trust the Lord?

I had a working knowledge of the truth, and I knew the truth would make me free from all this stuff. Even though I was in a lot of pain from this surgery and it took about three weeks for the last one to heal, I refused to look at any of these facts and circumstances. I looked to the Lord and I said, "Lord, I am not going to take these pain pills because you bore my pain at the cross, and I am going to trust you through this." Within three days I was healed with no pain and up and walking around. You choose: God's way or man's way? When I got out this time, I also only had five weeks of parole left because God knew what He was doing with my life, and He needed me to be free from everything so nothing could hold me back from going where He wanted me to go.

I also went back to work after I was healed, with the same people as before, only this time I had more of an influence over them than they had over me. I would take my Bible with me to work, and on breaks and lunchtime, I would read the Word and separate myself from them while they were getting high. My actions were a testimony to those guys because I was able to resist the drugs. They just didn't know I had no desire whatsoever to do drugs anymore. The taste for drugs was completely gone. After thirty-two and a half years of addiction, I was finally free. Going to prison didn't make me stop, being on parole and probation didn't make me stop, going to different twelve-step self-help programs didn't work for me. The only one who made me free was Jesus Christ! When I totally surrendered to Christ and allowed Him to come all the way in, He cast every demon out.

We can't depend on natural ways and self-help programs to deliver people from demonic strongholds that Satan has them in bondage to. Only Christ has the true authority to get rid of the demons. Get rid of the demon and the desire leaves with it. Overcome the temptation and the devil flees from you. Receive Christ as your "Higher Power" and study the Bible, and it will tear down the wrong thinking and set you on a path to recovery and freedom. Now that I was free and learning to be totally dependent upon the Master, He could start sending me places for His glory, to bring honor and glory to His name as a testimony to the truth that made me free.

Whenever I wasn't at work, I would be home spending time in the Word and with the Lord, getting intimate with the Father and honing in on His voice, communing, and conversing with Him. I still lived with my sister, but even in that environment, I lived for Him and Him alone.

One day while I was lying in my bed, just enjoying His presence in my room, He spoke to me and said, "I want you to go over to so and so's house." I replied, "Lord, I don't want to go over there, I'm weak when it comes to this stuff." He said, "I know you are weak, but in Me you are strong, now go." I said, "Okay, Lord, whatever you say." And out the door I went.

God had just asked me to go back to the very place where I used to sell drugs, do drugs, and hang out with a whole bunch of people whose lives revolved around drugs. When I got to my old friend's house, he wasn't at home but his girlfriend was. I knocked on the door, and when she answered, I didn't have to say a word. She took one look at me and said, "I heard you got out of jail a while back. You look different. You've been spending time with Jesus, haven't you?" I said, "Yes, yes, I have been." She said her boyfriend wasn't home, but she welcomed me in because she said he would be there any moment now.

No sooner than I got in the house and sat down, he came home from work. He knew I was there because he recognized my car out front of his home. He came in very glad to see me and said, "This is totally amazing that you are here because just today at work while I was on lunch, I started crying out to God for help to get off of these drugs, and I knew the Lord set you free so I told God if I could get a hold of you, then I too could get free." I asked what time was it when he was praying. He told me around twelve thirty or so. I said, "Dude, the moment you prayed God heard you, and He spoke to me while I was home in my room communing with Him. He told me to come over here to your house, or I wouldn't even be here right now."

Their jaws dropped open as they were standing there in awe of how fast God moved on his prayer. About this time, there was a knock on the door and three other people came in. It was the girlfriend's daughter and her two young adult sons. So now we had three generations of one family in the house. God knew what He was doing. He brought all these people together under one roof at this appointed time so they could meet Him.

All these people knew me and all we had known was the drug lifestyle. As a matter of fact, this place was in the middle of a community in the hills of West Virginia, and most of the people who lived here were on drugs in one shape, form, or another. Whether they were on prescription drugs from a doctor or illegal street drugs, a lot of people in this community were hooked and in bondage, but God was about to reach down and show forth His love by setting them free.

So in this house, as soon as everyone got seated in the living room, five people, three generations of one family were about to have heaven invade their home. I said, "Look, before we go any further, can I pray for you all?" They said, "Yes." That was good because as soon as I started praying, the presence of God filled that trailer. The Holy Spirit came in and did His work. I heard from heaven and said what the Father wanted me to say, and all five of these people surrendered their lives to Christ that day.

Then the grandmother said to me, "Please don't think I'm crazy or anything, but as you are sitting there and talking, I see this big yellow glow around your head." I said, "I don't think you are crazy. God is allowing you to see this thing so you know He is with me. These people were so touched and delivered by God that day that they practically begged me to come back and teach them about Jesus. They weren't ready to step into a church building, so we, being the church, must go to them, and I did just that. God took the house of these precious people, which was right in the middle of a drug community, and turned it into a house of prayer, praise, and worship. I started going over every Saturday and I took another friend from my church with me, and we would just allow the Holy Spirit to have His way in that place. We were making disciples of Christ, and the word started getting out how God was changing lives and setting people free.

One Saturday this other guy I know came in all high and drunk, just popped in. God brought him there because the Lord knew we wouldn't condemn him. I shared the Word with him and asked him if he wanted to be free from the alcohol and drugs. He said, "Man, I am sick of this life, and I am ready for something new." I said, "Jesus is who you need." He cried out, "Jesus, come into my life and help me." I knew he was sincere. I looked at the other guys in the house, the ones we'd been training in the ways of the Lord. I said, "Lay hands on him and command that spirit of bondage to loose him from these addictions." They did just that and God answered in a big way. Right on the spot, not only was he delivered, but God sobered him up instantly, so much so that the smell of beer and liquor even disappeared from him as God filled him with Himself.

He started jumping up and down and praising God. He said, "I came in here all high and drunk, but now I received Jesus for real in my life, and I can't explain how I feel, I am so clean feeling." And he ran out the door. We all looked at each other in amazement like, "what's up with that?" What we didn't know was that this guy was at a party up the road a little ways, and God brought him down to where we were to deliver him and set him free. He got so touched by God that he ran out the door and ran back up the street to the party and started giving testimony of what happened to him when the brothers prayed for him. He started telling them how Jesus set him free. We had no idea where he went when he ran out the door, but we were about to find out.

My friend from church and I got into my car about fifteen minutes after this guy ran out the door, and we had to go the same direction that he'd run off. When we got near the house where the party was, all these people came out into the street to stop us. I thought the same thing my friend spoke out of his mouth. He said, "What did we do here, what do these people want with us?" No sooner did he say that, I had to stop the car because they were blocking the street. They surrounded our car and one girl said, "Do to us what you did to him." She was talking about the guy who had just gotten set free. We got out of the car and I said, "We can't do anything to you. It is Jesus Christ who did this." They said, "Well, have Jesus do it to us. We are tired of being hooked on all these drugs." So we started to minister to them right then and there. Everyone of them received the Lord and what He had for them.

The grip of Satan was being broken off this community by the power of the Holy Spirit. When we yield to Him and do things His way, then powerful things happen, and He gets all the glory for what He is doing. We made disciples of Christ out of them outside of the church building, right where they were, and as they got free, they started to come into the churches with the fire of the Holy Spirit. It didn't matter to me if they came to my church or where they went because I taught them how to walk with Jesus and hear from Him and to go where He wanted them to go, to follow His plans and purposes for them, not mine.

One thing for sure was that they were saddened to hear that God was getting ready to change my location geographically. I heard from the Lord, "You are going to go to Miami Beach, Florida."

I said, "Okay, Lord, if you want me to go to Miami, then you need to make the way and supply the resources to get me there, and I thank you for sending me there." I didn't know anyone in Miami, but I knew if God said I was going there, then I was going and I knew He had prepared the way.

I told my family God was going to send me to Miami. They thought I was crazy. I'm getting used to people thinking that I am crazy because I follow the voice of God, but He has never let me down. I learned to trust in His voice, especially when He tells me things and I know that there is no way that I could accomplish these things in the natural. This way all I can say is that God did all this and He gets the glory in everything.

The more I surrendered to Him and humbled myself, the more He exalted me because He knew I would exalt Him. I found myself being placed in a leadership position in a Christian recovery program facilitated by our church. I was the facilitator of the male substance abuse group. I don't have any problems with twelve-step programs as long as they are Christ centered and established around the Word of God. All these things happened in a short span from me being released from prison. There are so many more testimonies of awesome things that God did in Maryland that I just don't have the space for it all, and I was only there for seven and one half months after I got out of prison.

How God brought me to Florida was a miracle in itself. One day I was eating at a restaurant, a guy who worked for a company that I had worked for while I was on work-release in prison saw me and told me that I should come over to his church because they had an evangelist up from Florida for the next two weeks. I didn't go that first night, but the Lord pressed me to go the second night. Not only were they having night-time meetings but they were taking people out on the streets during the day and training them to evangelize on the streets. This is my kind of ministry.

I went to the meetings and found out they had a ministry school in Miami Beach, Florida, and they were taking people in for the new school year in August. God said "Go." "Okay, Lord" was my reply. It was the spring of 2007 and the housing market was crashing, and I found myself out of work and my savings was running low and God was telling me to increase my giving. It didn't make sense in the natural, but when God says something, you just do it. We can't outgive God.

The closer it got for me to go to Miami, the less money it seemed that I had to get there and God is saying "Give, give, give!" The Bible says, "Give, and it will be given to you: good measure, pressed down, shaken together, and running over will be put into your bosom. For with the same measure that you use, it will be measured back to you" (Luke 6:38). I just trusted Him and His ways. Two weeks before I left for Miami, a twenty-thousand–dollar blessing came my way by way of workman's compensation for some kind of compensation when I was hurt and couldn't work. All I know is that God rewarded my obedience because I gave when He said to give and where He said to give. I didn't look at what I had when God kept telling me to give. I looked at who I belonged to and trusted that He knew better than I did.

One of my friends from church would make the journey with me, but before I left, I had a wedding ceremony in the privacy of my own room. I said to the Lord, "Father, you said in your Word that we are the bride of Christ so I marry myself to you, Jesus, and make my commitment to you a sure thing. Now, Lord, I am not looking for a relationship or anything like that because I make wrong choices when it comes to women. I always seem to pick the ones who will lead me astray.

But and if, Lord, you want me to be married, then you choose the woman and wife you have for me. She has to love you more than she ever will me. She has to have a passion for the lost and have the same calling on her life that you called me to, and she must like to travel since you called me to the nations."

I don't know why I prayed this prayer before I left Maryland, but I just knew I needed to commit this area of my life into His hands because He knows what is best for us.

So my friend and I left everything behind to follow Him. Off to Florida we went. It was July 29, 2007, exactly seven and one half months after I got released from prison. God also told me that one day I would be going back into the jails and prisons to minister. I was just following Him as He was leading, so Florida, here we come!

FOLLOWING THE SON IN THE SUNSHINE STATE

The Lord sent me to Miami Beach for His plans and purposes, not mine. The first week we lived in a motel until God showed us where He wanted us to be. Then He placed us in a neighborhood where there was a lot of drug activity and different gangs. We lived in this neighborhood for eighteen months, and by the time we left it, we had flipped it upside down for Jesus. My friend who had come to Florida with me went back home after six months, but my future wife lived in an apartment in the same building as I did, and it was she and I who reached out to this neighborhood. Plus, I had another guy living with me from Trinidad who was in Florida on a visa to attend the same ministry school.

I met my wife at the ministry school. God brought her down from Massachusetts at the same time He brought me from Maryland. He brought us together by the Spirit. Neither one of us was looking for a relationship. We were in the service of the Lord. So our whole life consisted of going to meetings together, ministering together, and seeking God together, but the Lord knew what He was doing. We were only at the ministry school for about four months because they were having some kind of problems and had to shut down in Miami Beach and move across the state, but the Lord told Katie and me to stay put in Miami. Katie is my lovely wife and partner in the ministry, but it would be about two years before we were married as God was drawing us together by His Spirit and doing a work in each of us.

After the ministry school shut down we continued doing street ministry. We would go down to Miami Beach and pray for people, bless them, and lead them to Jesus. We discovered where the Rescue Mission was and got involved with reaching out to the poor and homeless. We would pack bag lunches from our own resources and go out on the streets and feed the homeless. We started praying for people everywhere we went and witnessing to them about Christ. God started doing miracles right before our eyes. We saw God raise a few people out of wheelchairs—I'm talking about on street corners and parking lots. People were getting healed of HIV and incurable diseases. The greatest miracle is a transformed life and a soul that is redeemed.

Was our walk easy? Of course not. Some of the churches God led us to weren't exactly flowing in the power of the Holy Spirit, and we faced a lot of opposition because we were and they didn't want that tongue-talking, miracle-working power in their church. God would send us into these places to try to breathe new life into them. You can lead a horse to the water, but you cannot make him drink. We also connected to a lot of good churches who did recognize the gift of

God in us and wanted what we carried. All of these things were working together for our good as God was shaping and molding us for the work ahead and He continues to do so to this very day.

Did we do everything right and perfect? No, we didn't. We had opportunities and missed some of them. One day a lady broke her leg right up the street from where I lived, and I knew the Lord wanted to put that leg back together right on the spot because as soon as I committed to go that way the Holy Spirit gave me utterance in other tongues. I mean it just blurted out of me and the gift of faith was there to perform miracles, but when I got to where the ambulance was, I fell into fear and didn't do what the Lord wanted to do and it grieved the Spirit of God in me because He wanted out to do this miracle, but I suppressed Him by not speaking the Word of the Lord. I fell into self-condemnation after this, and it took a while for the Father to restore me out of this, not because of Him but because of me. I learned from this mistake and many others, that now, I'm at the point of no matter how ridiculous or hard something seems to be that the Lord ask of me, I will just do it.

We learned to stay faithful to what the Lord told us to do each step of the way. The Lord led us to connect with a traveling minister who had connections in the Vero Beach and Ft. Pierce, Florida, area. We came up to do a whole week of meetings at a church in Vero Beach and made other connections. After eighteen months in Miami, the Lord brought us to Fort Pierce, Florida. It was in early February 2009, and again, He planted us where the people needed Him most, and we just did our thing, street ministry. We reached out to them by sharing the gospel and praying for them.

Not long after coming to the Fort Pierce area, we met a prophetic minister and her daughter who are the pastors of a small congregation in Fort Pierce. The Lord also started moving us in a different direction than this other minister we were traveling with. He was planting us in this area to stay because He had a plan for us here to do and fulfill for His glory.

One day the Spirit of God told me to go down to this little prophetic minister's church because I was going to minister there on Sunday. I told the Lord that this minister can hear from Him very well, and that He needed to tell her that I'm coming because I'm not calling her, and He did just that. When Sunday came, the Lord asked me how bad did I want to minister, so I said, "Lord, you know I will do whatever you say," and He replies, "Well, you better start walking because no one is coming to pick you up." I had to walk about two miles to deliver what the Lord gave me to minister that night, and I had to walk that by faith because I trusted that the Lord told this lady I was coming. When I arrived there that night, she got out from her car and she told me that she did have a message prepared to give but that she believed the Lord wanted me to bring the message that night. I told her that He had told me the same thing. That one night turned into about three months of ministering on Sunday nights. My fiancee Katie brought the message a few of those times also.

God knew what He was doing. We just trusted Him and followed His leading. Our time was up with the traveling minister because God was planting Katie and me here in Ft. Pierce. God opened a door with a gentleman from this same small congregation, in which I am caretaker and maintenance man over his property and home in exchange for room and board. This has freed me up to do full-time ministry. This prophetic minister called me one day and said that the Lord told her to ordain Katie and me. She said the Lord told her we would need paperwork to get us into where God was about to send us.

Sure enough, we needed paperwork showing we were ordained ministers to get into the jail here in Ft. Pierce to minister. We've been going in to the jail for nearly two years at the time of this writing. God placed me in the home of a man who lived next door to the chaplain of the jail. The neighbor invited us to her home for Bible study on Thursday evenings and that is where we discovered what her husband did for a living. Before long we were welcomed into the prison ministry. The Lord was ordering our steps.

There were quite a few ministers, before the Lord led us to Fort Pierce where we were ordained, that wanted us to come in under them and go to ministry schools for a few years—to do things their way (the way they thought was the correct way) in order to be successful ministers and ordained. When I told them that the Lord wasn't leading me to do that, they told me that I would never make it in the ministry. They thought that I was rebellious. They didn't understand that I was following the voice of God. You judge for yourself: is it better to listen to God or to man? It's not by might or by power but by His Spirit. We went where the Father told us to go and did what He told us to do. Sounds a lot like the way Jesus lived His life.

> Then Jesus answered and said to them, "Most assuredly, I say to you, the Son can do nothing of Himself, but what He sees the Father do; for whatever He does, the Son also does in like manner. For the Father loves the Son, and shows Him all things that He Himself does; and He will show Him greater works than these, that you may marvel."
>
> John 5:19–20 (NKJV)

Katie and I married in July of 2009, and she moved into my home here in Ft. Pierce. Then God spoke to me that He was taking me back to Miami. I thought He meant to move there, but that wasn't so. He connected us with an apostle there and the Lord had us traveling back and forth to Miami every Saturday for a year, sitting under this apostolic ministry for further training in what He was preparing us to do. I had the privilege of going to Trinidad with this apostle for tent meetings, and it was training I'll never forget. We cast out demons every night of these meetings and watched as the power of the Holy Spirit healed, set free, and delivered people. I learned a lot from this man of God and I'll never forget my time with him.

I believe the Lord also had us making the almost two-hour drive from Ft. Pierce every Saturday to Miami for a year because He was preparing us for the road ahead. Since we have been called to the nations, the Lord was seeing if we could do a lot of traveling locally first without complaining.

Since we've gotten married, the Lord has sent us to the Bahamas. Of course that trip was also our honeymoon; however, many were ministered to on that trip because it is just who we are.

We've been back to Maryland where I shared my testimony in the recovery group that I had been a part of when it first started in my home church, and we saw revival break out in my own family as a lot of them were saved as they gave their hearts to Christ. A few even got baptized in water, and some in the Holy Spirit right in their own living rooms.

The kingdom of God is within us and Christ flows through us. We are just facilitators and extensions of His ministry. The Lord also reconciled me with my son on this trip as well, and we have been slowly getting to know one another. Nothing is too hard with God.

Our time came to an end from traveling back and forth to Miami because the Lord said we had learned what He had wanted us to learn. So we basically had meetings in our home because God said to do that while we were waiting on further instructions from Him. We met together every night, seeking Him through praise and worship and ministering to people wherever He led us to go.

Then He spoke to us to go to a fellowship in Lakewood Park, Florida, about ten miles from our house. The chaplain's wife had invited us to go, and we prayed about it because we just wouldn't go anywhere, if the Lord was not directing it. Several weeks later the Lord said, "Go." So we did, and we knew right away the Lord had us right where He wanted us to be once again. The church was a prophetic church. The first night we went the pastor said this in the middle of his message, "There's some of you here tonight that feel as if it's just you four and no more, and you've been meeting together in your living room because you're tired of church as usual. If that's you, then you're in the right place."

Katie and I looked at each other because we knew the Holy Spirit just spoke through this pastor directly to us. Also, the message he preached that night was a lot of the same things that God was showing us. I told the pastor that night that I liked the Word he brought forth because the Lord was speaking many of the same things to us. He looked at me and said, "The Lord is showing me that you are carrying something that the body needs to hear. Can you come back next week and minister here?" I said, "If the Lord wants me to, then I will be back." Well, the Lord sent us back and that was over eighteen months ago from the time of this writing, middle of 2012. We felt so at home in this place because there were no reins on the Holy Spirit. The pastors allowed Him to flow freely and they did ministry the way God told them to.

They received us into the fold and allowed God to use us in what He has called us to do. They didn't try to change us into their image but desired to see the image of Christ formed in us. Five-fold ministers and church leaders are called to teach, train, and equip the body of Christ to do the work of the ministry, and they did it well.

This is what the kingdom of God is all about—making disciples who will go into all the world. Those who will preach and demonstrate the love of Christ through signs, wonders, and miracles.

God exalted us while we were at this church. I say this not because of our accomplishments but because we humbled ourselves and stayed in that place of humility and did what God told us to do.

If God said, "serve another man's vision," then we did that. The key is to jump in with both feet and serve, support, and pray for the leaders God has placed you under. Serve along side them and then He will exalt you in due time. While serving we learned a lot about targeting and reaching a community for Christ. We learned a lot about the prophetic ministry, and God has taught us how to just really love Him more, and love people.

We were involved with jail ministry when we came to this church and now it is a part of the church. It all belongs to Christ and He's the one who sets us as stewards over the things He appoints us to do. As we faithfully came out to serve the pastor recognized us as the evangelists we are called to be and at the leading of the Lord we were placed in leadership over evangelism. We started evangelizing as a church body locally, and now as we have been faithful in that, God has opened the doors and made the right divine connections to send us to the nations of the world.

The doors swung wide open to us in the nation of Costa Rica. We witnessed God do some mighty powerful miracles in our meetings on this trip. A man came out of a wheelchair, cancer tumors disappeared, carpal tunnel was healed, bone diseases instantly gone, and many other things the Lord had done, but the greatest miracle is a transformed life and a soul that comes from the powers of darkness to the blood of Jesus and hundreds came to Christ through the Costa Rica ministry team.

As we serve, learn and grow, we know we will continue leading many different churches on mission trips around the world, all for the glory of God. The Lord has connected us with many different missionaries from all denominational backgrounds who we are laboring together with to do missions all over the world.

Even though we are part of this missionary network and we are at the beginning stages of our own ministry, D. O. C. World Missions, we are still able to serve in and through local churches. We believe we will always be able to serve in this capacity. This is what the kingdom of god is all about. We are all co-laborers together with God in Christ.

We really enjoy serving along side churches where the pastors, all the leaders, and the congregation have no problem taking it to the streets. People need to understand that we can't reach the world around us by keeping Christ contained in a building!

We minister and serve where the Lord sends us, it could be the local church, street corners, super markets, other countries or wherever, it doesn't matter. The kingdom of God is advancing and expanding. Who's willing to go? Surrender to Christ and He will take you on an exciting journey. I never said it would be easy, but stick with Him and it will be worth it!

United we stand, divided we fall. This is a time and season for the walls of division in the body of Christ to come down as He is preparing His bride for the wedding feast. A bride without spot or wrinkle. The harvest is plentiful but the laborers are few so we need to come together and go after the harvest. We shouldn't let differences, division, and denominational walls cause us to miss our place at the wedding feast of the Lord because He is calling people in from the highways and bi-ways. All who would come, the Lord says come!

THE FINISHING TOUCH

I wrote this book at the leading of the Holy Spirit, and without His encouragement, I don't believe I would have finished this work. This testimony of my life is to give hope to others who may find themselves trapped in a life of going around in circles with seemingly no way out. It's never too late to call on Christ Jesus to save you, heal you, and deliver you. Jesus himself said, "Behold, I stand at the door, and knock: if any man hear my voice, and open the door, I will come in to him, and will sup with him, and he with me" (Revelation 3:20). Will you open the door of your heart and let Him in today? I learned the most effective prayers are the ones from the heart. If you want Christ to come into your life to save you from your sins and forgive you for all you've done to sin against Him, then in your own words and from your heart, ask Him to come into your life. If you're not sure how to pray, then you could use the following as a guideline, but remember God wants it from your heart and not just lip service.

> Lord Jesus, I recognize that I've made one big mess out of my life because I am born into sin. I know and believe sin entered the world through Adam and this

was no fault of my own, but now that I know I am a sinner and that forgiveness for my sins can only come through you, I ask you to forgive me of my sins and to come into my heart. I know and believe that you are the Son of God and that you died on the cross, and that God raised you from the dead. You shed your blood so that I could be forgiven of my sins, and I receive your forgiveness and the gift of eternal life that you offer.

In Jesus's name I pray, Amen.

If that prayer was too long, then you might just cry out from your heart:

Jesus, I need you, come save me and help me.

Remember, it's not in our many words or eloquent prayers, but God wants the sincerity of your heart, and if you allowed Him to come in, then this is just the beginning of your new life in Christ. To deepen your relationship with Him, read the Bible to get to know Him better. Talk to Him by praying every day. Prayer is communication with God. Tell others about your decision to receive Christ and find a Spirit-filled church where you can worship, fellowship with other Christians and get involved with the church. Be sure the Bible is being taught and Christ is being preached.

If you have made a decision to follow Christ after reading this book or if it just inspired you and you want to connect with us we would love to hear from you.

Contact and connect with us:

D.O.C. World Missions Church
P.O. Box 4565
Fort Pierce, FL 34948
(772) 882-7156
www.docworldmissions.org

To contact Donald personally and/or want us to come and minister at your church or event, or you or your church are interested in missions, then you can e-mail me at d.nalley122@yahoo.com. SUBJECT: From Death to Life, or contact us through the D.O.C. World Missions website listed above.

May God bless everyone who reads this book and know there is always hope for you in Christ!

Also by Donald Nalley
"My Sheep Hear My Voice"

When God spoke to Moses He did so out of the flames of a burning bush. It was in the flames of a fiery furnace that three Hebrew boys weren't destroyed by the fire. John the Baptist declared that there was one coming after him who would baptize with the Holy Spirit and Fire. The Bible says God is a consuming fire. He will consume you but not destroy you. He wants to inflame you with a passion for an intimate relationship with himself. "My Sheep Hear My Voice" takes you on a journey of the simplicity of knowing you too can hear God's voice and be led by His Spirit.

Available at:
www.createspace.com
in paperback or amazon kindle

Also through the ministry at:
www.docworldmissions.org

"I AM THE WAY, THE TRUTH, AND THE LIFE. NO ONE COMES TO THE FATHER EXCEPT THROUGH ME"...

JESUS CHRIST

Made in the USA
Lexington, KY
29 November 2019